The Cambridge Introduction to
George Eliot

As the author of *The Mill on the Floss* and *Middlemarch*, George Eliot was one of the most admired novelists of the Victorian period, and she remains a central figure in the literary canon today. She was the first woman to write the kind of political and philosophical fiction that had previously been a male preserve, combining rigorous intellectual ideas with a sensitive understanding of human relationships and making her one of the most important writers of the nineteenth century. This innovative introduction provides students with the religious, political, scientific and cultural contexts that they need to understand and appreciate her novels, stories, poetry and critical essays. Nancy Henry also traces the reception of her work to the present, surveying a range of critical and theoretical responses. Each novel is discussed in a separate section, making this the most comprehensive short introduction available to this important author.

Nancy Henry is Associate Professor of English at the State University of New York at Binghamton. She is the author of, among other books, *George Eliot and the British Empire* (Cambridge, 2002; paperback edition, 2006).

Cambridge Introductions to Literature

This series is designed to introduce students to key topics and authors. Accessible and lively, these introductions will also appeal to readers who want to broaden their understanding of the books and authors they enjoy.

- Ideal for students, teachers, and lecturers
- Concise, yet packed with essential information
- Key suggestions for further reading

Titles in this series

The Cambridge Introduction to
George Eliot

NANCY HENRY

CAMBRIDGE
UNIVERSITY PRESS

CAMBRIDGE UNIVERSITY PRESS
Cambridge, New York, Melbourne, Madrid, Cape Town, Singapore, São Paulo, Delhi

Cambridge University Press
The Edinburgh Building, Cambridge CB2 8RU, UK

Published in the United States of America by Cambridge University Press, New York

www.cambridge.org
Information on this title: www.cambridge.org/9780521670975

First published 2008

Printed in the United Kingdom at the University Press, Cambridge

A catalogue record for this publication is available from the British Library

ISBN 978-0-521-85462-7 hardback
ISBN 978-0-521-67097-5 paperback

In Memoriam
George Brite Merchant (1920–2002)
Nancy Brite Merchant Henry (1929–2003)
Bitsy (1988–2005)

Contents

Preface

Two of George Eliot's fictional heroines fantasize about journeying to see a famous writer. Unhappy Maggie Tulliver in *The Mill on the Floss* harbors a pathetic dream: "she would go to some great man – Walter Scott, perhaps – and tell him how wretched and how clever she was, and he would surely do something for her" (*Mill*, IV:3). Equally wretched Romola leaves her husband with the intention of visiting "the most learned woman in the world, Cassandra Fedele, at Venice" to ask her advice about how she can learn to support herself (*R*, II:36). Perhaps the narrator of *Adam Bede* offers the explanation for why neither Maggie nor Romola realizes her fantasy: "if you would maintain the slightest belief in human heroism, you must never make a pilgrimage to see the hero" (*AB*, II:17).

George Eliot (Marian Evans Lewes) was a literary hero to many during her life and to subsequent generations of readers and writers. In historical memory, she is as compelling and charismatic a figure as she was in life. Her astonishing mind led men and women to fall in love with her even before she began to write fiction. Some fell in love with her through reading her fiction. In the final years of her life, many came to pay tribute at the carefully orchestrated afternoon salons in her London home, the Priory. After her death, some of the pilgrims became disillusioned, and her reputation suffered.

It is not surprising that 150 years since she published her first story, her fiction too has attracted acolytes and detractors, both with a peculiar intensity that reflects the ambivalent feelings of subsequent generations toward the Victorian age, which Eliot so powerfully represents. The realism that was praised in the mid nineteenth century for extending sympathy to common, unheroic people was often criticized at the end of the twentieth century for its essentially middle-class perspective. Such responses suggest that how we read George Eliot's writing has everything to do with our own historical context, but to appreciate her works properly, we need to know something about their contexts.

This book provides an introduction to Eliot's life, reading and historical milieu, contexts that are intimately related: reading was part of her life and her life is part of history. As her much-admired contemporary Elizabeth Barrett

Browning wrote in her verse novel, *Aurora Leigh* (1856): "The world of books is still the world" (Bk. 1, line 808). Interpretations of the individual works offered here may suggest some reasons why today's readers will find relevance to their world in Eliot's characters, her plots and the hard philosophical and moral questions they raise. The contexts make the texts more accessible so that readers may discover the intellectual and moral challenges – as well as the pleasures – of reading them.

Eliot's books remain popular, or perhaps more accurately, "canonical," generating editions, companions, and books and articles from a wide variety of critical perspectives. The proliferation of interpretations and scholarship is a testament to the richness – and to some extent the difficulty – of her writing. Scholarship adds to our knowledge, and criticism provokes our thinking; both are immensely helpful in exploring the complexities of Eliot's essays, novels, and poetry. The most compelling experience of her writing, however, will be personal, and will follow only from close, engaged, and informed reading.

Eliot's works speak to universal human experiences of the young and old: to misunderstood children, like Maggie Tulliver; to anyone who has lived with a secret, like Mrs Transome; to idealists, like Dorothea Brooke, who persist in bad choices with the best of intentions; to ambitious professionals like Tertius Lydgate, who become weighted down with petty politics and domestic cares; to women trapped in bad marriages like Romola and Gwendolen; or to those who have been adopted and wonder about their parentage like Daniel Deronda. Eliot's subtle, psychological portraits of these and many other characters account for the power her fiction still has today.

Just as Eliot's fiction showed – boldly for her time – that ordinary people could be the heroes and heroines of novels, so she knew that the great writer she had become, attracting pilgrims in want of advice, was really not a hero at all, but a fallible human being. The novelist Anne Thackeray Ritchie reported Eliot as asking, "if she hadn't been human with feelings and failings like other people, how could she have written her books?"[*] Perhaps this is why heroes should not be visited. Eliot knew that the best place to search for the wisdom of great writers was their writings.

---

[*] Quoted in Gordon Haight, *George Eliot: A Biography* (Oxford: Oxford University Press, 1968), p. 542.

Acknowledgements

I would like to thank Tom Cooper, Phil Rogers, and Margaret Wright for reading individual chapters of this book. I thank Graham Handley and Linda Bree for reading the entire manuscript. I have benefited from all of their comments. My ongoing conversation with Graham Handley about George Eliot's life and writing, begun over fifteen years ago, continues to provide insight and inspiration, and I thank him particularly for helping me to write an introduction to George Eliot.

Abbreviations

References to GE's works will be to volume and chapter numbers and the titles will be abbreviated as follows:

AB   *Adam Bede.* Ed. Valentine Cunningham (Oxford: World's Classics, 1996).

BJ   "Brother Jacob." *The Lifted Veil and Brother Jacob.* Ed. Helen Small (Oxford: World's Classics, 1999).

DD   *Daniel Deronda.* Ed. Graham Handley (Oxford: World's Classics, 1988).

FH   *Felix Holt.* Ed. Fred C. Thomson (Oxford: World's Classics, 1988).

GEL   *The George Eliot Letters.* Ed. Gordon S. Haight, 9 vols. (New Haven: Yale University Press, 1954–5, 1978).

LV   "The Lifted Veil." *The Lifted Veil and Brother Jacob.* Ed. Helen Small (Oxford: World's Classics, 1999).

Mill   *The Mill on the Floss.* Ed. Gordon Haight (Oxford: World's Classics, 1981).

MM   *Middlemarch.* Ed. David Carroll (Oxford: World's Classics, 1988).

Poetry *The Complete Shorter Poetry of George Eliot.* Ed. Antonie Gerard van den Broek (London: Pickering and Chatto, 2005).

R   *Romola.* Ed. Andrew Brown (Oxford: World's Classics, 1994).

Scenes *Scenes of Clerical Life.* Ed. Tomas A. Noble (Oxford: World's Classics, 1988).

SCW   George Eliot, *Selected Critical Writings.* Ed. Rosemary Ashton (Oxford: Oxford University Press, 1992).

SEPW   *Selected Essays, Poems, and Other Writings.* Eds. A. S. Byatt and Nicholas Warren (New York: Penguin, 1990).

SM   *Silas Marner.* Ed. Terence Cave (Oxford: World's Classics, 1996).

TS   *Impressions of Theophrastus Such.* Ed. Nancy Henry (London: Pickering and Chatto, and Iowa City: University of Iowa Press, 1994).

Chapter 1

Life

George Eliot's life provides as compelling a narrative as any she ever invented. Born the same year as Queen Victoria, the woman known successively as Mary Anne Evans, Marian Lewes, George Eliot and Mary Ann Cross lived through dramatic personal and cultural changes that track those of the nineteenth century. While George Eliot refused to sanction any biography during her life, she showed a lively interest in the biographies of others. After reading J. G. Lockhart's *Memoirs of the Life of Sir Walter Scott* (1839), for example, she wrote: "All biography is interesting and instructive" (*GEL*, I:24). Her novels are devoted to following the shape of her characters' lives. Just as she emphasized the significance of early events as clues to the psychology of characters such as Maggie Tulliver, Silas Marner, Tertius Lydgate, and Daniel Deronda, so her well-documented life experiences – of both her childhood and adult years – help us to understand her as a person and artist and provide insight into aspects of her fiction.

Mary Anne Evans was born on 22 November 1819 at South Farm on the Newdigate family estate of Arbury Hall near Nuneaton, Warwickshire, in that central part of England known as the Midlands. Her parents were Christiana Pearson Evans and Robert Evans. Christiana was Robert Evans's second wife and Mary Anne's family included two children from her father's first marriage (Robert and Fanny), as well as her sister Chrissey (b. 1814) and brother Isaac (b. 1816). While second marriages and stepsiblings were common in the nineteenth century, as today, the basic fact of this extended family is important to the portrayal of her fictional families, few of which are simple, nuclear families. Orphans, adopted children, and nieces and nephews living under the care of relatives occur in all of her novels except *The Mill on the Floss* (1860). In *Daniel Deronda* (1876), for example, Gwendolen Harleth is the daughter of her mother's first marriage, and tolerates her younger stepsisters with barely disguised disdain.

Christiana Pearson Evans died in February 1836 when Mary Anne was sixteen years old. Her health had been poor since the death of twin boys shortly after their birth in 1821. One may search the numerous mothers in Eliot's fiction

1

for clues to Christiana's character, yet these figures are contradictory: Milly Barton, Mrs Poyser, Lisbeth Bede, and Mrs Tulliver in the early fiction alone provide various forms of mothering. With little information offered by Eliot's letters, Christiana Evans remains elusive.

Much more is known about her father, Robert Evans, who played a central role in her life. An estate manager for the Newdigate family, he had responsibility for overseeing the tenants, the timber and various forms of land usage including coal mining. He acted as a liaison between the landholding and the working classes, an intermediary role that may shed some light on the origins of Eliot's own social and political perspectives. Her narrator Theophrastus reminisces about a Midlands childhood similar to Eliot's and a father who "knew very well what could be wisely expected from the miners, the weavers, the field-labourers, and farmers of his own time – yes and from the aristocracy" (*TS*, 2). It is clear that Eliot, like Theophrastus, considers those who have experienced the "mixed commonality" of our "national lot" to have a superior perspective on life generally (*TS*, 2).

Her father's privileged position allowed the young Mary Anne a glimpse of the life enjoyed by the landed aristocracy, and she had occasional access to the Newdigate library. She stored her observations from this period, incorporating them into her fiction, especially "Mr. Gilfil's Love Story" (1857), with its detailed description of the architecture and interior design of Arbury Hall [Cheverel Manor] and the earlier generation of Newdigates who had "Gothicized" the Tudor manor according to the late eighteenth-century fashion. The influence of this inside perspective on the landed classes is evident in the depiction of characters with an inherited sense of superiority, such as Arthur Donnithorne, Mrs Transome, Mr Brooke, and Sir Hugo Mallinger.

Eliot's memories of her life in Nuneaton and her companionship with her brother Isaac are most vividly recalled in her early fiction. For example, the town of Milby in "Janet's Repentance" (1857) is based on Nuneaton. In *The Mill on the Floss*, St. Oggs is based on Gainsborough and the river Floss on the Trent, but landmarks from her Midlands landscape (like the round pond) are transferred to this fictional composite. Her recollections of her father are incorporated in characters such as Adam Bede and Caleb Garth in *Middlemarch* (1871–2) – hard-working, morally upright men who attain the position of estate agent for wealthy employers.

The young Mary Anne was an excellent pupil at the girls' schools she attended and seems always to have had an intense intellectual life fueled by reading of all sorts and by the study of languages. Beginning with French in 1832, she learned (with the help of tutors) Italian, German, Latin, and Greek. Later in life she would acquire Spanish and Hebrew.

From 1828–1832, she attended boarding school in Nuneaton and became a favored pupil of her devoutly evangelical teacher, Maria Lewis. When she removed to the Misses Franklin's school in Coventry in 1832, she continued to correspond with Miss Lewis. The Franklin sisters were Baptists so that by this time she had come into contact with a variety of unorthodox religious views. In 1834, she underwent her own evangelical conversion and, for a while, all her intellectual energy was channeled into her reading of religious texts and her correspondence with Miss Lewis and a similarly religious friend, Martha Jackson. At times her ardor and renunciation bordered on fanaticism, and yet these letters show the future writer experimenting with metaphor:

> We are like poor creatures of whom I have read, who, for some cause or other, have been thrust out of the ship by their companions, try to grasp first one part of the vessel then another for support, until by the successive lashes that are given to make them loose their hold, they have no fingers left by which to venture another hopeless experiment on pitiless hearts. So we, having voluntarily caused ourselves to be cast out as evil by the world, are continually indicating a vacillation in our choice by trying to lean on some part of it within reach, and it is mercy that orders the lashing of our disobedient fingers, even though for a time we be faint and bleeding from the correction. (*GEL*, I:59)

Images of lashings and bleeding – in the tradition of the Passion of Christ – are frequent in her religious letters. In her fiction too she would not shy away from violent images of cuttings and torture as metaphors for mental anguish, albeit of a secular kind. At this time the Evanses were steadfast members of the Church of England. She exceeded their conventional beliefs and practices, and they thought her melodramatic and odd. But her piety and renunciations – of theatre, music, and novels – were tolerated because they were Christian and reflected the evangelical revolution within the Church of England.

In June 1841, Isaac married, and Robert Evans gave him Griff House where the family had lived since 1820. Mary Ann (who had dropped the "e" from her name) and her father took a new residence at Foleshill on the outskirts of Coventry. At least part of the intention of moving to a less isolated locale was to provide Mary Ann with opportunities for marriage, but the move had an effect quite unintended by her father, for here she struck up new friendships that were to transform her religious beliefs and open a new world of intellectual inquiry and fellowship.

She was already beginning to have religious doubts. At some point in 1841 she read Charles Christian Hennell's *An Inquiry Concerning the Origin of Christianity* (1838), a persuasively written treatise that was sympathetic to Christianity but concluded that there was no rational basis for belief in the miracles of the New Testament. In Coventry, Mary Ann found an environment in which she could debate and discuss such ideas, which would have been neither understood nor tolerated by her family or her religious friends. Her developing friendships with the local ribbon manufacturer Charles Bray, his wife Cara, her sister Sarah Hennell, and brother Charles Hennell, author of the *Inquiry*, led to a new regimen of reading in non-religious literature and exposure to progressive intellectual and social thinking among the guests at the Bray's home in Coventry. As a result, she experienced what might be called a reverse conversion as she began to question and eventually reject formal Christianity. Just as she had gone too far for her family in her religious fervor, so now she went too far in her scruples about practicing a religion in which she could no longer believe.

The story of Eliot's intellectual, religious, and political development is an interesting combination of susceptibility to influence by friends like Miss Lewis and the Brays, and an independence that set her at odds with specifically patriarchal authority (her father and brother). This is a combination of traits that she shares with Maggie Tulliver, and which, more than any situational parallels between Eliot's life and that of her heroine, shows why *The Mill on the Floss* may be considered a partially autobiographical novel.

Her refusal to attend church with her father and friend Maria Lewis on 2 January 1842 was a profound experience in her intellectual and emotional development, primarily because she came to repent this "Holy War." She later saw the damage she had done by not compromising her principles for the sake of her personal relationships, regretting that she had caused pain and dissension.[1] And yet, her intense desire to pursue truth and knowledge, as well as personal fulfillment, would lead to further rifts with her family and her past. According to Rosemarie Bodenheimer, the most astute reader of Eliot's letters: "The incident established her intellectual and moral honesty, her understanding that such honesty would be socially misunderstood and punished, and her need to expiate or redeem the consequences of her unconventional intelligence through sacrificial service."[2]

For the next several years, she performed the duties of an unmarried daughter to her widowed father, even attending church, but her intellectual expansion continued. She took over from Charles Hennell's wife Rufa the task of translating David Strauss's *Das Leben Jesu* (1835–6) as *The Life of Jesus, Critically Examined*. In completing this demanding labor, she brought one of the foremost examples of the historical biblical criticism called the German Higher Criticism to English audiences. The book examines the life of Jesus as told in the four Gospels, finding evidence for the origins of the story in myths rather than in history. It applied a rational, scientific method to its study of texts that Eliot, who already viewed the Scriptures as "mingled truth and fiction" (*GEL*, I:128), also saw as great literature, and dissecting the beautiful story of the Crucifixion depressed her (*GEL*, I:206). Yet characteristically, she fretted over every detail to produce an impressive translation, which was published anonymously in 1846.

Meanwhile, Charles Bray purchased the radical newspaper, *The Coventry Herald and Observer*, and she began to contribute essays and reviews so that reading, writing, and discussions with friends rendered the daily caring for her demanding father less oppressive than it might otherwise have been. She was rewarded by the sense of fulfilling her duties, especially in her father's last year when he required constant nursing. At the same time, her mind had transcended the limitations of her country upbringing and she was longing to see the world beyond her Midlands home.

Upon Robert Evans's death at the end of May 1849, she set off with the Brays to enjoy the experiences of foreign travel that would eventually become central to her intellectual and creative life. After traveling to France, Italy, and Switzerland, she parted with her friends, electing to stay in Geneva and live alone for the first time (July 1849–March 1850). Drawing on her small inheritance, she passed the time reading, people-watching, and getting to know the family in whose home she lodged, the D'Albert Durades, who remained life-long friends.

When she returned "home," she found herself outcast and unhappy amongst her family, and having had a taste of independent living, decided to try London. The significance of her decision to move to London cannot be overestimated. Young women in mid-nineteenth-century England did not do such things. She commented that it always surprised her when people found her being alone odd (*GEL*, I:301), and she would not allow other people's opinions now, or later, to deter her from pursuing her desire to be at the intellectual center of the country, indeed – at this time – of the world.

In London, she lodged at 142 the Strand, office and home of John Chapman, friend of the Brays and publisher of progressive books, including her own translation of Strauss's *Life of Jesus*. He had recently purchased the *Westminster Review*, a periodical that had a long history of advancing liberal thought. The enthusiastic, over-committed Chapman was at a loss how to regenerate the journal as a newly important medium of intellectual debate. Marian (as she now called herself) had contributed her first of many reviews to the *Westminster* in January 1851 (of R. W. Mackay's *The Progress of the Intellect*). Chapman recognized the extraordinary talents of his lodger and invited her to become his editorial assistant, the (unacknowledged) editor of the journal.

Marian Evans acted as the editor of the *Westminster Review* – without formal credit or pay – from 1851–1854, an intellectually exciting and emotionally turbulent period. Chapman's domestic life was as chaotic as his professional life. He lived with his wife, children, and the children's governess who was also his mistress. Despite becoming entangled in a romance with Chapman that put her into conflict with both his wife and mistress (and which sent her temporarily packing to Coventry), she kept her focus on work. She wrote a Prospectus for the journal and was responsible for keeping it at the forefront of mid-Victorian intellectual life. This work introduced her to the leading thinkers of the day.

At a meeting on 4 May 1852 to protest price fixing among publishers, for example, she was the lone woman in the room where Charles Dickens, the scientific and sociological theorist Herbert Spencer, novelist Wilkie Collins, naturalist Richard Owen, and others made speeches and discussed a strategy to oppose the attempts of large publishing houses to squeeze out competition from smaller operations, such as Chapman's.[3] During this period, she also met the most important women on the intellectual scene, including the widely accomplished and published author Harriet Martineau and the early advocates of women's rights, Bessie Rayner Parkes and Barbara Bodichon. Bodichon would become perhaps her closest friend in the years ahead.

As her flirtation with Chapman was cooling into a professional relationship, she found herself drawn to Herbert Spencer. Then an editor at the *Economist*, he would become a major proponent of evolution theory, coining the phrase "survival of the fittest" usually associated with Darwin. She had a brief, intense emotional involvement with him, which ended in July of 1852 with his rejection of her affections (at least partly on the grounds of her physical unattractiveness). Meanwhile, she was coming to respect and admire Spencer's friend and *Westminster* contributor George Henry Lewes, a highly intellectual and versatile journalist, playwright, actor, drama critic, and novelist with a growing interest in natural science.

Lewes's domestic life was, like that of so many Victorians, irregular. When he first met Marian, he was still living with his wife, with whom he had three sons. Agnes Lewes had become involved with her husband's best friend, Thornton Hunt, who had his own wife and children. The two men co-founded the radical periodical, *The Leader* in 1850 and continued to publish in the midst of their interpersonal entanglements. It is thought that by the time Lewes moved out of their home in 1852, Agnes had had two children with Hunt, though Lewes signed as father on both of their birth certificates (1850 and 1851).

Although the facts about this period of their lives are obscure, biographer Rosemary Ashton believes that they became intimate at the end of 1852 or beginning of 1853.[4] In October 1853, Marian moved out of Chapman's house and into her own lodgings. In December 1853, she resigned as editor of the *Westminster*. Work continued on the *Leader* and she contributed a number of reviews, helping Lewes to meet deadlines in April 1854 when his poor health prevented his working. She was also translating another important German work of Higher Criticism, Ludwig Feuerbach's *Das Wesen des Christenthums* (1841) as *The Essence of Christianity* (1854), which had a strong influence on what has been called her religious humanism or sometimes her "religion of humanity," a term originating with the contemporary French philosopher, Auguste Comte (1798–1857). For Feuerbach, who took an anthropological approach to analyzing Christianity, religion was fundamentally human rather than divine, answering human needs and projecting human ideals as deities to be worshipped. Feuerbach argued that the essence of Christianity should be found in human relations, a notion that George Eliot would emphasize repeatedly in her fiction as well as in her justifications for the course she and Lewes were about to follow.

In July 1854, Eliot and Lewes took the momentous step of traveling together to Weimar, Germany in a gesture that announced their intention to live together as a couple. This dramatic act began for both of them a period of intellectual and social enlightenment. Lewes pursued research for his groundbreaking English biography of the great German poet, novelist and man of science, Johann Wolfgang von Goethe (1749–1832), while both wrote review essays for the *Westminster* and other English periodicals that helped fund their travels. The unmarried couple enjoyed a honeymoon of social acceptance in a European community of artists and intellectuals that included the composer and pianist Franz Liszt and which was much more tolerant of their relationship than the censorious circle of gossiping friends and acquaintances they had left behind.

But both of their lives were in London and return was inevitable. The scandal they had evaded by leaving confronted them upon their return. Eliot stayed alone in Dover, working on a translation of the seventeenth-century Dutch-Jewish philosopher Baruch Spinoza's *Ethics*, while Lewes went to find lodgings for them close to London. Eventually they settled in Richmond as the Leweses, a fictional identity to which they would adhere for the rest of their life together.

While today the decision of two mature adults to live together in a committed relationship seems unexceptional, for the time it was a radical gesture that served to alienate and isolate the woman from social respectability much more than the man. Marian was not "received," even by her own and Lewes's acquaintances, and she clung to her belief in the moral rightness of this relationship based on love rather than legal marriage to sustain her through a difficult period when most people regarded her as a woman living in sin. It is important to note that she did not set out to flaunt her independence or to defy the institution of marriage, though she had always been skeptical about the "noose of matrimony" (*GEL*, I:54). Rather, she was insistent that the true marriage was one of minds and of affections regardless of legal status.

It was not long before the professional benefits of her decision to stay with her intellectually compatible partner became apparent. She wrote several long review essays for the *Westminster*, including "The Natural History of German Life" (1856) and "Silly Novels by Lady Novelists" (1856). Lewes encouraged her to try her hand at writing fiction, and during a period when she accompanied him on his scientific research trips to various coastal locales in Britain (including Tenby in South Wales, the Scilly Isles, and Jersey), she set herself the task of writing stories. With his numerous connections in the publishing world, Lewes proved invaluable to getting his partner's work published. He contacted John Blackwood, the editor of the *Blackwood's Edinburgh Magazine*, and told him about a friend who was writing fiction that might appeal to the journal's audience. Lewes delivered Marian's "clerical scene," "The Sad Fortunes of the Reverend Amos Barton," to Blackwood in November 1856. All contributions to *Blackwood's* appeared anonymously, but in this case, even her editor and publisher did not know her identity. Yet he astutely recognized talent in this mysterious new author and so played along when, in February 1857, "he" identified himself as George Eliot.

"Amos Barton," "Mr. Gilfil's Love Story," and "Janet's Repentance" were serialized between January and November 1857. *Scenes of Clerical Life* was published as a book in 1858 under the pseudonym George Eliot. It immediately stirred up interest and controversy, not only in London, but also in Nuneaton where residents speculated about the identity of the author and about "originals" for characters in the stories. Isaac Evans had no way of knowing that his sister was writing about some of their former acquaintances and would soon become famous through novels that drew even more explicitly on family memories, but he was suspicious of a letter in which his sister informed him of her marriage to Lewes. He had his solicitor ask for particulars of the marriage and she was forced to admit that it was not a legal union. Just as she was finding success as an author, the break with her family became complete. They stopped writing to her and she was never to see any of her siblings again.

Rather than follow through with her plan to write more scenes, she decided to take a "broader canvas" (*GEL*, II:381) for what she described to Blackwood as "a country novel – full of the breath of cows and the scent of hay" (*GEL*, II:387). She began *Adam Bede* in October 1857 and progressed rapidly. By the time the novel was published in February 1859, she was already at work on another.

The combination of humor and drama in this carefully observed portrait of rural English life during the Napoleonic wars made *Adam Bede* a critical and commercial success, its first edition selling out in a matter of weeks. George Eliot's popularity soared as did curiosity to know "his" identity.

Marian Lewes was dogged in her success and desire to preserve anonymity by the public claims that George Eliot was a Nuneaton clergyman named Joseph Liggins. Initially the Leweses joked about this claim published in the *Manx Sun* (July 1857), but the rumors became annoying when they turned Liggins into a victim who had gone unpaid for his writing. London's literary set was divided between pro and anti-Ligginsites. While everyone involved preferred to keep her identity anonymous, she was eventually compelled to admit that George Eliot was Marian Evans Lewes, sparking a new round of gossip about the woman living with George Henry Lewes.

Meanwhile she was writing her intensely personal next novel, which she had thought to call "Sister Maggie" or "The House of Tulliver." She paused in the composition of the novel to write "The Lifted Veil" (1859), whose dark, misanthropic tone may reflect her bitterness over the public's behavior in the Liggins matter as well as her sensitivity to criticism about her unmarried status. In September 1859, she and Lewes traveled to Gainsborough, finding that the town and the river Trent would serve well as models for the setting she had in mind for the new novel. In January 1860, Blackwood proposed a title, *The Mill on the Floss*, which, despite its inaccuracy (the mill is actually on the Ripple), had a sound that all parties liked.

By the time of the publication of *The Mill* (1860), Eliot's estrangement from her past had become a settled fact. Her identity was now that of a voluntary exile who could not go home again. Gradually, her writing took new directions that were not tied to memories. In March of 1860, she and Lewes set off for Italy where they pursued an energetic regimen of sightseeing. In Florence, Lewes suggested that the life of the Dominican monk Girolamo Savonarola (1452–98) and his brief rule over the city at the end of the fifteenth-century might make a good subject for an historical novel. Eliot took to the suggestion, but not before writing a short story, "Brother Jacob" (finished in August 1860) and beginning another English novel in September. This would become *Silas Marner* (1861). Following its appearance, she and Lewes returned to Italy for further research on the historical novel, *Romola*.

The Italian novel proceeded through a great deal of research to recreate late fifteenth century Florence. *Romola* was a departure in many ways. She accepted a lucrative offer from the publisher George Smith (initially £10,000) to publish in the *Cornhill Magazine*, thus leaving Blackwood, who felt personally betrayed. Writing to monthly deadlines for the serial publication in a magazine was stressful; the material was difficult emotionally as well as factually to get right. *Romola* was her only real commercial failure, though some critics appreciated the remarkable historical and psychological accomplishment it represented. She offered Smith "Brother Jacob" for free as consolation for *Romola*'s losses, and when it was time to write her next novel, she returned to Blackwood.

That projected novel would also return to her favorite setting – England in the previous generation – and would use the first Reform Bill of 1832 as an indirect means of reflecting on the current debates about what would become the second Reform Bill of 1867. *Felix Holt* (1866) is not usually considered one of George Eliot's more artistically successful novels, but its complex inheritance plot integrates separate stories in a way that anticipates *Middlemarch*, her greatest work. The juxtaposition of an older generation (Mrs Transome, Rufus Lyon) living with the consequences of its choices and a younger generation (Harold, Esther and Felix) struggling with its own moral choices, shows both an aesthetic and personal maturity. She was now writing from the mid-point of a life when she had made her choices, for example to live with Lewes and act as stepmother to his sons, who were now making their way in the world.

In the 1860s, Eliot began to experiment with poetry, some of which was published. One idea she had been contemplating since 1864, originally as a drama, was an historical tale of fifteenth-century Spain and of the heroic actions of a woman who learns that she is descended from Gypsy royalty. Like Elizabeth Barrett Browning's verse novel *Aurora Leigh* (1857), the epic, book-length poem that became *The Spanish Gypsy* (1868) is a coming-of-age story and a romance. Rather than realizing her identity as an artist, like Aurora, Fedalma answers her calling to lead her exiled people to a new homeland. Lewes and Eliot traveled to Spain to research this story, which looks back in its exotic setting to *Romola* and forward in its themes of cultural identity and nation building to *Daniel Deronda*.

In May 1863, when Eliot was contemplating the two stories, "Middlemarch" and "Miss Brooke," which eventually merged to form the novel *Middlemarch*, Lewes's son Thornie, who had left England for Natal, South Africa, full of hope and energy early in 1863, returned in an appalling physical condition. Their letters, as well as Lewes's daily journal entries, tell the sad story of Thornie's wasting away from what is thought to have been spinal tuberculosis. He died in October 1869 at the age of 25, passing away, according to Lewes, in the arms of his stepmother. She had felt close to the dying young man, the process of caring for him no doubt recalling her final year of nursing her father. She wrote in her journal for 19 October 1869: "This death seems to me the beginning of our own."[5] Amazingly, she channeled this grief, wisdom, and perspective into what was to become her masterpiece.

In *Middlemarch*, Eliot reached the apex of her assurance and authority as a novelist. The ambitious vision of providing a study of provincial life – rather than the life of a central character – was realized with a knowing and controlling yet sympathetic and seemingly objective eye and voice. The finished whole was rewarded with critical and commercial success. The Victorian critic Sidney Colvin astutely remarked on the relationship between the contemporary narrative voice and the 1829–32 setting that whereas "the matter is antiquated in our recollection, the manner seems to anticipate the future of our thoughts."[6]

It wasn't long after the publication of *Middlemarch* that Eliot began to contemplate her next novel. *Daniel Deronda* is first mentioned in Lewes's journal of 1873 as a play. By the fall of 1874 she had begun writing it as a novel. As they had done with *The Mill on the Floss*, the Leweses scouted locations that would help her to describe precisely the various settings she had in mind. They settled on Henry Fox Talbot's Lacock Abbey as a model for Sir Hugo Mallinger's estate, Topping Abbey. Fox Talbot was the English pioneer of photography and the modernity of his experiments set in contrast to the medieval architecture of his residence provide a fitting background to the themes of her novel. Among the novel's many allusions to technological advancements in the 1860s is a sly reference to the modern vogue for photographic visiting cards. Compared to Gwendolen, the heiress Miss Arrowpoint: "immediately resembled a *carte-de-visite* in which one would fancy the skirt alone to have been charged for" (*DD*, I:5).

The setting of *Deronda* is the closest to contemporaneity of all Eliot's novels and the only one representing London and the fashionable upper-middle class and aristocratic society with which she had become acquainted in the years following her success as a novelist when, not surprisingly, the legal status of her marriage became less of a barrier to her taking a place at the dinner table. As usual, it also encompasses the lives of the lower middle classes, for example the household of the Meyrick women in Chelsea and the pawn-broking establishment of the Cohens in Holborn.

The satirical treatment of the Victorian equivalent of the jet-set (this set traveling with ease by the railroads that were not yet available to the characters in her earlier novels) was influenced by her trips to a variety of European and English spas where she and Lewes frequently sought cures, particularly for his persistent maladies. Their trip to Bad Homburg in 1872 is thought to have inspired the memorable gambling scene that opens the novel.

As her anthropological interest in the transient, cosmopolitan society she had observed – as well as her desire to write about it – grew, so did her intellectual interest in Judaism. The research she conducted into Jewish traditions for *Deronda* was inspired by her friendship with the scholar Emanuel Deutsch, from whom she took Hebrew lessons and through whom she became intrigued with the idea of a Jewish return to Palestine. Deutsch, who clearly provided a model for her sickly visionary Mordecai, died en route to the holy land in 1873.

George Eliot's position as England's greatest living novelist, solidified by the publication of *Middlemarch*, enabled her to take the unorthodox step of presenting a detailed, sympathetic portrait of English Jews in tandem with a condemnation of the direction she thought English Christian culture and society were taking. The novel was met with criticism, and some lamented her departure from the subject of the rural, English past. But perhaps in their nostalgia, they overlooked the critical eye she had turned on that past in her treatment over the years of alcoholism, child-murder, ignorance, poverty, and narrow-minded conventionalism.

In the last years of her life, Eliot became a kind of icon, whose reputation was bolstered by her Sunday afternoons at the Priory, where she received worshipful visitors. Elma Stuart (1837–1903) loved her passionately and was buried beside her. Edith Simcox (1844–1901) kept a journal in which she referred to Eliot almost as a kind of deity. This view of Eliot as a wealthy, bourgeois establishment figure and representative of Victorian morality unfortunately colored her reputation after her death, as those who saw her then wrote memoirs and accounts that often left out her role as a progressive thinker and aesthetic innovator dedicated to representing the lives of ordinary, commonplace, often-disenfranchised Britons.

After the publication of *Deronda*, the Leweses became unavoidably preoccupied with their own physical health. Over the years the two had endured an unending series of physical ailments, which they recorded in their journals and letters. Now, both were suffering more than ever – she from kidney pains that were a premonition of her death – and he with gastro-intestinal problems that were symptoms of the cancer that would kill him. Yet neither let up in their irrepressible drive to learn, read, and write. They sought refuge from London, and in December 1876 were able to purchase a country house, called the Heights, at Witley in Surrey. Here, in the last two summers of their life together, he pursued work on his multi-volume scientific study, *Problems of Life and Mind* (1874–9) and she wrote what was to be her last book, *Impressions of Theophrastus Such* (1879), an experimental departure from her previous fiction reflecting on her role as a creator of characters and unknowingly foreshadowing the fragmented, allusive nature of Modernist writing. She finished *Theophrastus Such* shortly before she and Lewes returned to London in the fall of 1878, and one of his last acts was to send the manuscript to Blackwood.

Lewes died on 30 November 1878. Understandably, Eliot was inconsolable and refused to see anyone for months, with the exception of Lewes's surviving son Charles and eventually their friend John Walter Cross. Also understandably, given her tireless work ethic, she threw herself into the project of completing Lewes's unfinished *Problems of Life and Mind*. Before she could consider re-entering the world of the living, she saw these volumes through to publication and dedicated herself to seeing that Lewes received the recognition he deserved as a scientific thinker.

It was Cross, a long-time family friend and financial advisor, who finally broke through to the widow in her grief. The forty-year-old, unmarried man had lost his mother within days of Lewes's death. The unlikely result of their communion was his proposal of marriage to the woman he previously had called "aunt." She accepted and the two were married on 6 May 1880. They took a honeymoon journey to Europe, which ended disastrously with Cross's mysterious mental breakdown in Venice. They returned to England and bought and furnished a home on Cheyne Walk in Chelsea. Before they had time to enjoy their home or their married relationship, Eliot died, probably of kidney disease, on 22 December 1880, aged 61.

Cross soon found that because of her agnosticism and her irregular relationship with Lewes, Eliot was not entitled to the burial in Westminster Abbey's Poet's Corner that befitted her position as the greatest of Victorian novelists. She was instead modestly buried next to Lewes in Highgate cemetery.

For much of her life, George Eliot enjoyed biographies. By 1879, however, she seemed to resist the very idea of biography: "The best history of a writer is contained in his writings – these are his chief actions" (*GEL*, 7:230). She must have discussed the treatment of her life's story with Cross because the three-volume biography that he went on to write – and that shaped his wife's reputation for years to come – is really a carefully controlled autobiography in that much of it consists of Eliot's own words, and tellingly, it is the author George Eliot's life that is announced in its title rather than that of Marian Evans or Lewes or Cross – names most readers would not even have recognized. Through careful editing (and occasional distortions), *George Eliot's Life as related in her Letters and Journals*, arranged and edited by her husband J. W. Cross (1885) solidified her image as a moral paragon: a genius yes, but also a didactic and rather humorless person. Anyone who reads her work closely and appreciates the verbal play and strong, pervasive sense of humor could not accept this as a final portrait of the artist. It took years to overthrow the weight of this Victorian biography. The recovery of her independent, original, and unorthodox contribution to English literature is still in progress.

Chapter 2

Historical contexts

In *Felix Holt*, George Eliot wrote, "there is no private life which has not been determined by a wider public life" (*FH*, I:3). All of her works situate her characters' lives in relation to the broader social conditions – or context – of their times. Similarly, we must understand her writing within the public context of nineteenth-century society and culture. In determining which of the virtually limitless aspects of nineteenth-century life and thought are most relevant to the interpretation of her work, we may take our clue from the texts themselves. In order to comprehend what Eliot's works achieved and conveyed in their time – and therefore to appreciate them in our own – we need a basic knowledge of four interrelated categories: religion, science, politics, and culture.

Many of Eliot's works are set in the early decades of the nineteenth century, the period of her parents' rather than her own adulthood. With historical hindsight, she was able to explore the influence of the immediate past on the present generation, including on herself. This past is described in *Impressions of Theophrastus Such* by a narrator/author whose Midlands childhood was similar to that of Mary Ann Evans, including a conservative father "born much about the same time as Scott and Wordsworth" who spoke nostalgically about the good old days:

> Altogether, my father's England seemed to me lovable, laudable, full of good men, and having good rulers, from Mr. Pitt on to the Duke of Wellington, until he was for emancipating the Catholics; and it was so far from prosaic to me that I looked into it for a more exciting romance than such as I could find in my own adventures . . . (*TS*, 2).

Here Theophrastus describes Eliot's own practice of looking back to the period between the administrations of Prime Ministers William Pitt the Younger (1783–1801) and the Duke of Wellington (1828–30), setting her realism and her romance – with the exceptions of *Romola* and *Daniel Deronda* – during the span of her father's life (1773–1849).

Theophrastus observes further: "Certainly that elder England . . . has great differences from the England of to-day. Yet we discern a strong family likeness"

(*TS*, 2). The metaphor of family likeness to describe the relationship between past and present goes far toward explaining Eliot's choice of historical settings in her fiction and also her conception of history and society. Like the great spokesman for English conservatism, Edmund Burke, Eliot believed that the present is bound to the past as to a parent and is at least in part determined by it. In *Reflections on the Revolution in France* (1790), Burke wrote: "People will not look forward to posterity, who never look backward to their ancestors."[1] While Eliot did not share in Burke's defense of the aristocracy and lament over the loss of chivalry – in *The Mill on the Floss* she refers to "Burke's grand dirge" (*Mill*, IV:3) – all of her works caution implicitly that change must occur slowly so that society may adapt and that traditions must be respected for the continuity they provide individually and collectively.

In *Adam Bede*, set during the Napoleonic Wars, Adam is chagrined with his fretful mother, as he had been frustrated by his alcoholic father. The narrator steps in to explain his feelings: "Family likeness has often a great sadness in it. Nature, that great tragic dramatist, knits us together by bone and muscle, and divides us by the subtler web of our brains; blends yearning and repulsion; and ties us by our heartstrings to the beings that jar us at every movement" (*AB*, I:4). Adam, Maggie Tulliver, and Romola all try to break ties by physically leaving home; all are compelled by conscience to return. The family-likeness analogy for the relationship between past and present carries some of the same implications. We are responsible for not cutting our roots abruptly and violently. We must look at the family likeness if we are to understand how we are the same and how we are different from our parents and their generation. Eliot's conception of childhood differs from Wordsworth's in most ways, but overall, her fiction affirms his paradoxical formulation in "Ode: Intimations of Immortality from Recollections of Early Childhood" (1807): "The Child is Father of the Man." In reading her novels, we need to be aware of the social context of the time in which each work is set, the later social context in which it was produced, and the relationship between the two.

Religion

Felix Holt begins with a description of a stagecoach ride "five and thirty years" before the novel's publication in 1866. Coaches had been replaced by trains as a means of traversing the country, but the narrator is nostalgic for the more scenic form of travel and uses the imagined coach ride as a way to paint the changes between the past and present and also between different geographic regions in the 1830s. In the agricultural parts of the Midlands, there were no

Catholics to be found, but the inhabitants "were saved from the excesses of Protestantism by not knowing how to read, and by the absence of handlooms and mines to be the pioneers of Dissent" (*FH*, Introduction). In contrast, the next stage of the coach's journey finds the landscape dotted with "the gables of Dissenting chapels" and the atmosphere altered by "the breath of the manufacturing town" (*FH*, Introduction). This connection between the material circumstances of weavers, miners, and factory workers, and their attraction to "dissenting" religions, figures in the plots of "Janet's Repentance," *Adam Bede, Silas Marner, Felix Holt* and *Middlemarch*. To understand such references – intended to introduce the climate of social and political reform in the 1830s – as well as to understand the fundamental plots and themes of her works, we need to review the basic structure of the Church of England in the nineteenth century.

High Church, Low Church, Dissent

The Church of England, or Anglican Church, was established by King Henry VIII in 1534. In breaking with the authority of the Pope and making himself the head of the church, Henry consolidated and strengthened his own power (not to mention authorizing his own divorce). This initial break with England's Catholic tradition opened the door to Protestantism and subsequent religious and political strife in which the Church struggled with Catholics and Puritans to keep its hold on the monarchy. Following the beheading of Charles I, the English Civil War, the Puritan Commonwealth of Oliver Cromwell, and the restoration of the monarchy in 1660, the Test Act of 1673 required holders of civil and military offices to be Anglicans. When the Catholic James II acceded to the throne and then fathered a son – threatening a Catholic dynasty – it led to an (invited) invasion in 1688 by an army led by the Dutch Protestant Stadholder William of Orange and the establishment in 1689 of William and Mary (Protestant daughter of James) as King and Queen of England and Scotland. After this "Glorious Revolution", a royal lineage was established that guaranteed a Protestant monarchy with Catholics and Dissenters excluded from the avenues of national power.

There were of course many varieties of Protestantism within and outside of the established church. By the nineteenth century, those whose beliefs and practices were closest to their Catholic origins were known as High Church Anglicans, while those who deviated furthest from the rituals and ceremonies of Catholicism but remained within the Anglican fold were known as Low Church. Those in the middle were called Broad Church. The evangelical revival established Methodism in the 1730s and continued to have influence in a variety of forms through the early nineteenth century, including a fundamentalist, reforming movement within the Church itself. Amos Barton in *Scenes of Clerical Life* is a Low Church cleric whose minor reforms (such as stopping the singing in Shepperton Church) make him unpopular with his parishioners. The Reverend Tryan in "Janet's Repentance" is an evangelical clergyman who goes further, offering unorthodox Sunday night sermons that attract the poor – "just like a Dissenter" – and in which he preaches that good works are not necessary for salvation. To intolerant men like Robert Dempster, Tryan's "praying with old women, and singing with charity-children" smacks of radicalism (*Scenes*, I:1). Dempster launches a campaign of harassment and intimidation against the well-meaning outsider. Eliot knew from her own experience how divisive religious differences could be. She told Blackwood in June 1857 that Tryan's persecution was "a real bit in the religious history of England that happened about eight-and-twenty years ago" (*GEL*, II:347), but her fiction shows that ignorance and intolerance posed a greater threat to social stability than variations of religious doctrine.

Groups whose views empowered the individual (as opposed to the clergy) to interpret Scripture to a degree that was incompatible with Anglican orthodoxy and the privileged hierarchy it entailed, were known as Dissenters. This democratic extension of spiritual power to the people was precisely what made Dissent appealing to the disenfranchised and impoverished working classes in the rapidly industrializing cities and explains why the "gables of Dissenting chapels" were evident wherever there were handlooms and coal mines. Dissenting sects, including Unitarians, Baptists, Methodists (like Dinah Morris in *Adam Bede*), and independent congregations, such as the church in Lantern Yard to which Silas Marner belonged, complicated and politicized the religious scenario of the nineteenth-century. Catholics (with their strong tradition in Ireland), Presbyterians (with their foothold in Scotland), and Jews (expelled from England in 1290 but readmitted by Oliver Cromwell in the 1650s) further contributed to the mix of beliefs and practices making up the population in nineteenth-century, officially Anglican Britain.

There was also a movement to return the church to many of its Catholic rituals (without acknowledging the Pope's authority). Known as the Tractarians for their series of publications, *Tracts for our Times* (1833–41), members of the Oxford Movement, as it was called, instigated an influential, rather elitist push toward conservative reform within the church that stirred debate and controversy. In "Amos Barton," "the effect of the Tractarian agitation was beginning to be felt in backward provincial regions" and the "vibration of an intellectual movement" led to the monthly clerical meetings described in the story

(*Scenes*, I:2). The Church of England remained the state religion and, in Eliot's fiction, is the institution to which most characters belong.

As we have seen, Mary Anne Evans was raised in the Church of England. At home, her father and brother had High Church leanings. Separated from her family at the various boarding schools she attended, she came under the influence of evangelical and dissenting Christians such as Maria Lewis who seemed to speak to her own unorthodox way of thinking and to her intense moral and spiritual needs. She became attracted to a particularly severe, Calvinist form of Chistianity, though she remained within the Church of England.

Eliot's correspondence from her early life is primarily with evangelical friends, Lewis and Martha Jackson. As Rosemarie Bodenheimer has shown in *The Real Life of Mary Ann Evans*, she was always conscious of her audience when writing letters. These letters reveal a piety and devotion that seem extreme, but it is clear that she was discoursing with her friends in an insular private language (including the assignment of coded names) so that her fervor is as much an exercise in rhetorical expression and role-playing as an indication of her beliefs and practices.

In addition to her own enthusiastic personal faith, George Eliot was aware of the structure and the politics of the Anglican church. The clerical hierarchy would have been familiar to anyone growing up in the heart of rural England in the early and middle decades of the nineteenth century. She chose the role of the clergy in Midlands society as the unifying theme for *Scenes from Clerical Life*, but by the time she wrote *Scenes*, she had moved far beyond her youthful evangelicalism. She emphasized the humanity of clergymen, the saving influence they might have on members of a community, and in turn that members of a community might have on them. In this sense, the men who found careers in the national institution of the church and played their part in every community in England were more important to her recreation of English society than the content of their beliefs.

Clergymen are important in her fiction from the three central characters in *Scenes of Clerical Life* (Barton, Gilfil and Tryan) to Reverend Irwine in *Adam Bede* and Reverend Stelling and Dr Kenn in *The Mill on the Floss*. In the latter, as throughout her work, she balances cynicism about the clergy – evident in her subtle but biting portrait of the social-climbing Mr Stelling and his wife – with respect for the well-intentioned, even if ineffectual Dr Kenn. In *Felix Holt*, the High Church Reverend Debarry looks down with intellectual and class bias on the Dissenting, socially unimportant Rufus Lyon. In *Middlemarch*, Mr Cadwallader is a jolly cleric with a prosperous living who is primarily concerned with fishing. Mr Casaubon similarly enjoys the prosperity of a well-to-do parish but is absorbed in his (primarily pagan) *Key to All Mythologies* and performs his clerical responsibilities rather soullessly. Mr Farebrother is a good man but unsuited for his clerical career, as Fred Vincy would have been had he followed his father's wish that he enter the church. Mr Gascoigne in *Daniel Deronda* is exposed to Eliot's critical eye, summed up in the narrator's aside that as Captain Gaskin he had taken "orders and a diphthong" to improve his social and material standing in the world.

To appreciate how George Eliot arrived at her secular view of the clergy requires an understanding of the broader cultural critique of Christian belief that came from within England and also from European influences, particularly the historical criticism of the Bible known as the German Higher Criticism. Eliot was at the forefront of this challenge to accepted belief and became instrumental to its dissemination when she published her translations of Strauss's *The Life of Jesus* (1846) and Feuerbach's *The Essence of Christianity* (1854).

God and the Bible

The church was an established fact of nineteenth-century English life. It provided careers for young men as a state institution, and even in its diversity and divisions underpinned a uniform national identity. In the Victorian period, however, a questioning more radical than that of church doctrine was occurring. Not just a matter of who could interpret Scripture but the very authority of the Scriptures themselves – and by extension the authority, even the existence, of God – came into question. For many Victorians, especially the highly educated, this doubt was profoundly unsettling. Some, including Eliot's contemporary authors Matthew Arnold and Alfred Tennyson, grappled with their doubt in poetry. Through her fiction, Eliot searched for alternatives to religion – for reasons to act morally other than obedience to God or fear of His punishment.

It would be difficult to underestimate the radical nature of the new approaches to examining the Bible that emerged in the nineteenth century. Eliot's turn away from evangelicalism was the product of personal soul-searching, the application of reason to what she had previously taken on faith, and of her reading and contact with radical friends. Her abandonment of faith in religion and in God coincided with a larger movement that assaulted the institutions and beliefs of her society. The approach of thinkers such as Charles Christian Hennell, Strauss, and Feuerbach is rightly called critical. It may also be called scientific in the sense that it subjected sacred texts to the scrutiny of rational principles.

Eliot's conversion from Christianity in the 1840s took place just before the publication of Robert Chambers's anonymously published, controversial, and widely popular *Vestiges of the Natural History of Creation* (1844) and well before Darwin's *On the Origin of Species* (1859) contributed to what is often viewed as the Victorian crisis of faith. Eliot and Lewes read Darwin's book immediately and its presence may be felt in the novel she was writing at the time, *The Mill on the Floss* – in the animal metaphors, the language of natural selection and the overall portrayal of Maggie as a "mistake of nature" who is not fit to survive in the environment of St Ogg's. The reverberations of Darwin's work would continue to be felt in society at large and in her fiction.

Natural science

In Victorian periodicals such as the radical *Westminster Review*, which Eliot edited, and the conservative *Blackwood's Edinburgh Magazine*, in which her first fiction appeared, literature, politics, and science were not the separate fields of knowledge that they are today. Contributors and readers had an interest in all aspects of contemporary thought, and the journals reflected these interests. Natural science – the study of the natural world including geology, chemistry, biology, and human physiology – were all of general interest. Such subjects were in the process of branching off into professionalized fields of specialized knowledge, and at mid century "science" still included what we would now call pseudo-sciences, such as phrenology (advocated by her friend Charles Bray), Mesmerism and Spiritualism (which Lewes attacked in print).

Eliot had an abiding interest in all new scientific thinking, and her relationship with Lewes brought her directly into contact with the latest scientific developments. She wrote *Scenes of Clerical Life* while living with him and hunting for marine specimens for his *Seaside Studies*, a popular account of his research combined with a survey of the latest literature on the topic. The 1830s vogue for collecting specimens in a strictly amateur capacity is evident in Eliot's portrayal of Mr Transome in *Felix Holt* and of Mr Farebrother in *Middlemarch*.

By the 1850s, the distinction between amateur and professional scientist was beginning to emerge and contention for authority was becoming fierce, fought out in the pages of journals, pamphlets, and books, as well as in the establishment of professional societies. Lewes, who had no university education, was vulnerable to charges of amateurism. As editor of the *Westminster Review*, Eliot tried to suppress a critical review of Lewes's book, *Comte's Philosophy of Sciences* (1853), written by Thomas Huxley (who would become known as Darwin's bulldog) and accusing Lewes of amateurism. *Middlemarch* treats early moves towards professionalization as the educated newcomer Lydgate attempts to reform the antiquated practices of the town's doctors. Borrowing scientific language for its subtitle, "A Study of Provincial Life," the novel incorporates metaphors of the microscope, telescope, and stethoscope to scrutinize English provincial life, while tracing Lydgate's career, research, and personal life.

At the level of language and metaphor, as well as in the plot, scientific reform is central to the novel, which also questions the ways in which technology is applied. Eliot's fiction at times implies that heightened perceptions of sight and sound do not in themselves produce new knowledge. Just as she implicitly cautioned against such preternatural powers in her fantastical story "The Lifted Veil," so in *Middlemarch*, the narrator is grateful that human beings cannot hear the squirrel's heart beat or the grass grow, and Eliot's attitude toward technological advancements – despite the enthusiasm she shared with Lewes for his microscopic investigations – remained skeptically cautious to the end. All of Lydgate's "galvanizing" of animal parts, dissections, and studies under the microscope lead him to mistaken conclusions about human pathology.

Technology

One of the first things Eliot did when she moved to London was to visit the 1851 "Great Exhibition" at the Crystal Palace. Itself a remarkable architectural construction of iron and glass, the Crystal Palace became a showcase for the latest technologies from around the world, especially from Britain, which was leading the nineteenth-century industrial and scientific revolutions. Her fiction, with the exception of *Daniel Deronda* and *Impressions of Theophrastus Such*, is set too early to incorporate or examine these new technologies, but part of her careful historicizing involved showing the impact of whatever technology was new at the time of her narratives' settings. *The Mill on the Floss* (set 1829–39), for example, refers to new technologies of land irrigation and to the coming of steam engines to turn Guest and Co.'s mills as Mr Deane tells Tom: "It's this steam, you see, that has made the difference: it drives on every wheel double pace and the wheel of fortune with 'em" (*Mill*, VI:5).

Eliot was born before the first railway lines were laid. She took her first journey by train in 1839. By the time of her death railways covered Britain and the European continent, and her ability to travel extensively depended on them. She also invested her money in foreign, colonial, and domestic railway companies, thereby contributing to railway construction around the globe. *Middlemarch* describes the first steps of surveying the land for the laying of a line into the town. In the face of opposition, questions arose about whether such life- and land-altering technology was in fact "progress." Perhaps her character Caleb Garth speaks for her when he sensibly tells the laborers who attempt to stop the preliminary preparations for the railroad: "Somebody told you the railroad was a bad thing. That was a lie. It may do a bit of harm here and there, to this and to that, and so does the sun in heaven. But the railway's a good thing" (*MM*, VI:41). Eliot's position on technological advancements was balanced and ambivalent. In *Felix Holt*, while preferring the coach, her narrator projects beyond the railroads: "Posterity may be shot, like a bullet through a tube, by atmospheric pressure from Winchester to Newcastle: that is a fine result to have among our hopes; but the slow old-fashioned way of getting from one end of our country to the other is the better thing to have in memory" (*FH*, Introduction).

In March 1878, Eliot and Lewes saw the newly invented telephone "explained and demonstrated" (*GEL*, VII:16). By then the world seemed to be introducing innovations and advancements at every turn. "Shadows of the Coming Race" in *Impressions of Theophrastus Such* entertains the idea of machines taking over society. Cannily and comically, it combines the latest in technological inventions with the then-established idea of human evolution. Theophrastus hears of "a microphone which detects the cadence of the fly's foot on the ceiling, and may be expected presently to discriminate the noises of our various follies as they soliloquise or converse in our brains – . . ." (*TS*, 17). Recalling Latimer's powers in "The Lifted Veil" to hear the thoughts of others, he compares his response to that of an "unfortunate savage too suddenly brought face to face with civilization . . .". He asks: "Am I already in the shadow of the Coming Race? And will the creatures who are to transcend and finally supersede us be steely organisms, giving out the effluvia of the laboratory . . ." (*TS*, 17). This dystopian and ironic vision of the future makes it clear how pervasive technology was at the end of Eliot's career and how seriously she considered the consequences of a society transformed by new scientific ideas and machines. As John Picker points out, at her death she had completed the opening section of a new manuscript set during the Napoleonic Wars; offering her characteristic present-time hindsight, the narrator explains: "This story will take you if you please into Central England and into what have been often called the Good old times. It is a telescope you may look through a telephone you may put your ear to: but there is no compulsion."[2] A telephone to the past becomes a wonderfully apt metaphor for the recreation of past speech for an author who claimed she heard her characters speaking.

The closely related issues of religious and scientific reform and the progress of thought and technology in Eliot's life and writing were also connected to political reform, which she saw shaping the future of the nation and about which she remained similarly cautious and skeptical – alternately hopeful and despairing about the direction her country was taking.

Politics

Politics – broadly interpreted – are central to Eliot's fiction. The major social movement with which her fiction is concerned is social and political reform. In the nineteenth century, the passion to reform institutions, laws, and even personal behavior touched every aspect of society, from the abolition of slavery in the British colonies (1833) to the removal of disabilities (or prohibitions on civil rights such as the ability to hold office) for Dissenters (1828), Catholics (1829), and Jews (1858). In her time she also saw the advancement in women's rights and improvements in education, health and sanitation.

In *Felix Holt* and *Middlemarch*, she addressed the challenges posed to class hierarchy by political reform. For Eliot, like her radical Felix Holt, the granting of voting rights was secondary to the fundamental problem of education. What good would it do to extend voting privileges to those unequipped to exercise them responsibly? She applied a similar critique to women's rights, believing that the extension of the franchise, or right to vote, to women could only be effective when women were educated enough to make informed choices. This reluctance to support progressive legislation put her at odds with her reforming female friends like Barbara Bodichon, but she was more in sympathy with efforts to establish Girton College, the first Cambridge college open to women, assuring Bodichon that the better education of women was "one of the objects about which I have *no doubt*" (*GEL*, IV:299).

Perhaps Eliot's disaffection from movements to extend the franchise stemmed not only from what she called the conservative turn of her mind and her solidly middle class (and increasingly wealthy) status, but also from her exclusion, as a woman, from the political process. What did the political views of a woman signify in mid-Victorian England, even those of a popular, critically respected and highly paid female novelist? As Harold Transome tells his mother, it does not matter what women think because "they are not called upon to judge or act" (*FH*, I:2). However, Harold's views reflected his society in 1833, a time with few opportunities for women, as both *Felix Holt* and *Middlemarch* emphasize. By her own age Eliot felt some small progress had been made. At the same time that she could be devastating in her critique of the various ways in which society can destroy women or socialize them to destroy themselves – think of Milly Barton, Hetty Sorrell, and Maggie Tulliver – she thought the progress of women, like all social change, should occur slowly and naturally without damage to the fabric of society.

By the Victorian period, England's constitutional monarchy and limited democracy was – like the governments in the UK and US today – primarily a two-party system. At the start of the nineteenth century, Tories or Conservatives were identified with the landed, aristocratic interest and the Whigs or Liberals with the new-monied, middle-class interest. In 1830, a Whig government under prime minister Earl Grey came into power for the first time in fifty years and began pushing for political reforms that would redistribute representation to reflect a nation in transition from a rural to an industrial economy with a population increasingly concentrated in cities. The Whigs wanted more members of Parliament to represent the burgeoning industrial cities and fewer for the depopulated (rotten or pocket) boroughs "presented by noblemen desirous to encourage gratitude" (*TS*, 2). The right to vote was based on ownership of property. Reformers also wanted to lower the property requirement for voting. Far from universal suffrage, this would turn only one in seven adult males into voters.

Middlemarch is set just before the passing of the Reform Bill of 1832 and *Felix Holt* just after. In the latter, it is expected that Harold Transome, like his neighbor Philip Debarry, will stand for his district as a Tory in his family's tradition, but Harold shocks everyone by declaring as a pro-reform Radical. In undertaking this position, Harold is not only breaking with tradition but working against his own interest as a landholder. In advocating the dilution of landed power by increasing the voting pool, he is viewed as a traitor to his class. Similarly, in *Middlemarch* the landowning Mr Brooke shocks his neighbors by coming out as a vaguely positioned Independent candidate.

Agitation from the growing and increasingly organized working classes pressured the movement for reform, at times over the course of the century threatening violence and raising the specter of revolution that so haunted British society following the American and French Revolutions. In representing politically-motivated mob behavior in "Janet's Repentance," *Felix Holt* and *Middlemarch* (all set in the Midlands during the 1830s), Eliot seems to be invoking not only riots that actually occurred when the House of Lords initially defeated the Reform Bill, but also threats to social stability from events that occurred outside the time frame of her fiction, such as the Chartist demonstrations in favor of working class rights during the 1840s as well as social revolutions throughout Europe in 1848. Her only explicit, published views about political developments in her own time came in the "Address to the Working Men, by Felix Holt" (1868), an anomalous piece she published at the urging of her publisher John Blackwood that employs the persona of Felix Holt to comment on the second Reform Bill of 1867 and cautions newly enfranchised working men about the difficulty of true reform, which must come from education not just voting. He warns them against the divisiveness of class interests and advises them of their solemn responsibility to vote for the good of everyone, not just themselves: "None of us are so ignorant as not to know that a society, a nation, is held together by . . . the dependence of men on each other and the sense they have a common interest in preventing injury" (*SCW*, p. 342). As a woman unable to take part in the political process and as an artist concerned with the place of her art in society, Eliot was less interested in political parties than in urging the nation to examine, define and improve itself.

Empire and nation

During Eliot's life, Britain was a dominant colonial power. In the days of George III (1760–1820), when works such as "Mr. Gilfil's Love Story," *Adam Bede*, and *Silas Marner* are set, the American colonies had been lost (1776) and reforms such as the abolition of the slave trade (1807) had turned the British colonial impulse in other directions, especially toward India. The Indian Empire was an established part of Victorian life. The Indian Mutiny, or Sepoy Rebellion, of 1857 resulted in the government taking over from the East India Company to rule the colony. Eliot and Lewes knew colonial administrators: their friend Edward Bulwer Lytton was made Secretary of State for the Colonies in 1858 and his son Robert, also a close friend, became Governor-General of India in 1876. The Indian Civil Service, like the Church of England, provided employment opportunities for young men, and Lewes's son Thornie aimed to enter the service but failed the examination. As a result, Thornie and his brother Bertie emigrated to the British colony of Natal in South Africa. References to colonial careers appear in Eliot's work, as in most Victorian fiction. "Brother Jacob" exposes the ignorance with which a young Englishman sets off to Jamaica in search of an easy life. In *Daniel Deronda*, Rex Gascoigne fantasizes about emigrating to Australia, while his brother Warham, more practically, enters the Indian Civil Service. By this time, however, both Thornie and Bertie had died after failing to prosper in the colony, so that Eliot knew intimately the uncertainties and dangers of the colonizing process.

The various aspects of colonial and imperial rule pervaded British society and culture. The globalizing effects of colonialism and imperialism on Britons at home and abroad helped to shape Eliot's advocacy of European nationalist movements and of Jewish nationalism toward the end of her life. In "The Modern Hep! Hep! Hep!," the title of which refers to a medieval Crusader cry that finds modern expression in anti-Jewish sentiments, Theophrastus argues that the "idea of Nationalities" has value because it preserves distinctions that give groups their identities. Such national identities have become a modern trend: "That any people at once distinct and coherent enough to form a state should be held in subjection by an alien antipathetic government has been becoming more and more a ground of sympathetic indignation" (*TS*, 18). Eliot wrote in an era that saw the emergence of new states (Greece, Germany, Italy), and while England was not a new nation, the act unifying Ireland with Great Britain (England, Scotland and Wales) dated only from 1801. Since that time free trade, emigration and immigration were changing the character of the nation and portending a "fusion" of the races. In *Felix Holt*, Harold returns from Smyrna with a son whose mother was a Greek slave. By the time she wrote *Deronda*, she was more concerned than ever with asking readers to consider what, after all, made them British.

Daniel Deronda, with its pointed critique of the rootless, cosmopolitan European classes and the earnestness with which it represents Daniel's search for both a personal identity and a larger collective mission, is the novelist's attempt to pose this question for her readers. National identity is forged in national memory and maintained by the preservation and transmission of those memories in the form of culture. Eliot, in her role as re-creator of a national past and as a generator of a distinct art for her time, was instrumental to defining British culture during the Victorian period.

Culture

In the 1850s, Eliot's essays and early fiction were concerned with establishing a realist aesthetic in opposition to contemporary fiction that she found lacking in its commitment to realistic representation. Her impressions of the failures of Victorian fiction were staked out in her 1856 essays "The Natural History of German Life" and "Silly Novels by Lady Novelists." She wrote during a time when the realist fiction of Dickens, Thackeray, Trollope and Gaskell contended with the sensationalism of authors like Wilkie Collins and Mary Elizabeth Braddon, as well as with the prevailing melodramatic tendencies of Victorian drama. Dickens, with his extensive theatrical experience, often resorted to melodrama in his fiction. Lewes, also with a theater background that included acting with Dickens, came to oppose the use of melodrama in fiction.

In conjunction with essays by Lewes, such as "Realism in Art: Recent German Criticism" (1858) – which called for just the sort of fiction she had begun providing – Eliot defined her work in strategic contrast to that of her contemporaries.

With her wide-ranging intellectual and aesthetic sensibilities, she was inevitably a product of her times and was responding continually (whether positively or negatively) to the artistic innovations that characterized mid-Victorian culture.

She was an accomplished musician and a lover of all forms of classical music. In Germany, she and Lewes attended early operas by Wagner, *Lohengrin* and *The Flying Dutchman*, and she wrote about them in "Liszt, Wagner, and Weimar" (1855). According to Eliot, Wagner believed that opera must be "an organic whole, which grows up like a palm" (*SCW*, p. 86). In this sense, his notion of opera is consistent with her sense of fiction, as implied from the organic model of form she develops in "Notes on Form in Art" (1868): "The highest Form, then, is the highest organism, that is to say, the most varied group of relations bound together in a wholeness which again has the most varied relations with all other phenomena" (*SCW*, p. 356). But she objected to the lack of melody in Wagner and playfully takes her metaphors of natural science further:

> It is just possible that melody, as we conceive it, is only a transitory phase of music . . . We are but in "the morning of the times", and must learn to think of ourselves as tadpoles unprescient of the future frog. Still the tadpole is limited to tadpole pleasures; and so, in our state of development, we are swayed by melody.   (*SCW*, p. 87)

The quotation is an excellent example of how she thought about art in other mediums, expressed herself through fantasies of evolutionary development (which she was still doing in her last book, as in "Shadows of the Coming Race"), and quoted with ease from her contemporaries (Tennyson's poem "The Day-Dream"), all to stress a serious point about a modern musical innovator whose career paralleled hers. In 1877, Wagner gave a series of concerts at the Royal Albert Hall in London where the Leweses met him and his wife (Cosima – daughter of their friend Franz Liszt) frequently.

Adam Bede establishes that she took Dutch painting as a model for her realism (*AB*, 17), but she was also extremely interested in contemporary art, including the pre-Raphaelite school. She did not have much opportunity to write art criticism *per se*, but she did review Ruskin's *Modern Painters* (1856), with which she had a profound affinity with respect to realist principles: "The truth of infinite value that he teaches is *realism* – the doctrine that all truth and beauty are to be attained by a humble and faithful study of nature" (*SCW*, p. 248).

Eliot's fiction is interestingly placed in relation to the Victorian debates about the state of English society and culture. Matthew Arnold saw culture as the antidote to the decline of modern society, the gap left by the abandonment of religious faith and the moral uncertainties facing an industrialized and commercialized society moving into a new world. In *Culture and Anarchy* (1869), he advocated the importance of diffusing "the best knowledge and thought of the time" and contributed to an ongoing conversation about the "condition of England" and the state of modern culture that included works such as Carlyle's *Past and Present* (1843) and Ruskin's *Unto this Last* (1862).[3] Eliot was not as dramatically worried about the corruption of the "cash payment nexus" (in Carlyle's terms) as some of her contemporaries were. She and Lewes did not neglect the business side of her authorship and her income as a female author (or worker of any kind) was unique. She did, however, distinguish herself whenever possible from authors who wrote for money only, and this distinction is crucial to her identity as an artist.

She began with a desire to communicate to a broad popular audience, writing to Blackwood when he had questioned the appeal of "Janet's Repentance" that she "should like to touch every heart among my readers" (*GEL*, II:348). With *Scenes of Clerical Life* and *Adam Bede* in particular, she succeeded in this ambition. But after *The Mill on the Floss* – with its insistence on the necessity of representing the everyday life of unexceptional, even vulgar, people – the internal arguments for this imperative begin to fade. After the erudite and commercially unsuccessful *Romola*, she became less concerned with communicating with the many and more focused on creating great art with a disregard for the advantages of writing best sellers. Referring to her epic poem, *The Spanish Gypsy*, she asked Cara Bray: "Don't you imagine how the people who consider writing simply as a money-getting profession will despise me for choosing a work by which I could only get hundreds where for a novel I get thousands?" (*GEL*, IV:439).

In the Victorian period the distinction between popular and critically acclaimed literature was not what it came to be in the early twentieth century when authors and critics looked upon popularity as incompatible with the production of great art. Dickens is perhaps the best example of a novelist whose work was consistently popular and praised by his own and later generations of critics. *Middlemarch* is a fine example of a novel that was popular (though not as popular as *Adam Bede*) and yet has been recognized by generations of critics as a great artistic achievement.

Once she no longer needed to worry about money, her mission as an artist changed from representing the common people realistically to pushing the novel's limits and scrutinizing national behavior. In *Deronda*, she did this with intersecting narratives: the dreamy, idealized plot of Deronda and Mordecai and the hard, realistic social critique of Gwendolen and Grandcourt. Some found the novel baffling at the time and into the twentieth century some critics wanted to rend the Gwendolen from the Daniel part. But today we can see how the writer who helped establish the realist novel as the dominant Victorian genre was moving aesthetically at the end of her life toward an experimental, impressionistic style. Thematically, she discovered in Jewish culture a satisfying – even model – form of identity and national belonging that England seemed to lack.

In recreating the world of the previous generation, her novels strove to archive her own and her nation's history. In contrast to the Jews, the English had a spot of native land in reality and not just in memory. In contrast to the Irish, the Indians or the Chechnyans, that home had not been invaded or held by an "antipathetic government" since the Norman Conquest. Her hope was that her novels would help readers revere their traditions while correcting the errors of the past. She would have her readers make the past part of the present, part of themselves.

Chapter 3

Literary influences

As we have seen, before and after Mary Anne Evans became George Eliot, reading was an essential part of her life. The fact that she read more widely than any other Victorian novelist – as well as the often densely allusive nature of her writing – means that identifying the major "influences" on her work is particularly complex and challenging. In recent years literary critics have tended to approach the connections between literary works as questions of "intertextuality," detecting linguistic similarities that reflect broader cultural discourses. When attempting to understand Eliot's writing in the context of her life and times, the more literal notion of influence can be a useful part of that historical contextualization. This chapter will concentrate on a set of literary texts that pervade her writing and implicitly or explicitly influenced both its style and content.

Eliot gained proficiency in Greek and Latin – a notable accomplishment for a woman who could not attend the universities where young men pursued their studies of classical languages and texts. It is not surprising then that she made the exclusion of a girl from a classical education and the folly of force-feeding Latin to a boy central to the first book of *The Mill on the Floss*. In trying to explain the psychological harm inflicted on Tom Tulliver by Mr Stelling's insistence that he swallow an uncongenial and impractical curriculum of geometry and Latin, Eliot's narrator tells us that Tom was as uncomfortable "as if he had been plied with cheese in order to remedy a gastric weakness which prevented him from digesting it" (*Mill*, II:1). Unsatisfied with this image, the narrator apostrophizes the Greek philosopher Aristotle (384–322 BCE), author of *The Poetics*, a text that instructed his contemporaries and centuries of later writers on the fundamental principles of poetic and dramatic composition:

> Oh Aristotle! if you had had the advantage of being 'the freshest modern' instead of the greatest ancient, would you not have mingled your praise of metaphorical speech, as a sign of high intelligence, with the lamentation that intelligence so rarely shows itself in speech without metaphor, – that we can so seldom declare what a thing is, except by saying it is something else? (*Mill*, II:1)

Her reference to *The Poetics*, while playful, shows how self-conscious she was about her increasingly experimental use of metaphor and about her prerogative as a modern to disobey classical constraints.[1]

In the *Poetics*, Aristotle defines metaphor as "giving the thing a name that belongs to something else."[2] In his discussion of tragedy, he argues: "But the greatest thing by far is to be a master of metaphor. It is the one thing that cannot be learnt from others; and it is also a sign of genius" (Ch. 22). Aristotle advises using metaphors in moderation and cautions against using them "with a view to provoking laughter" (Ch. 22). Eliot seems to defy his advice by using metaphors extensively, trying on one and then another with the intention of provoking laughter: Tom's mind is a field to be cultivated, an intellectual stomach, a blank slate, and a mirror. Meditating on the effects of changing the metaphor and also on Tom's obliviousness to metaphor generally, she concludes: "Tom was in a state of as blank unimaginativeness concerning the cause and tendency of his sufferings, as if he had been an innocent shrew-mouse imprisoned in the split trunk of an ash-tree in order to cure lameness in cattle" (*Mill*, II:1).

In *The Mill*, Eliot lets loose her metaphoric powers, delighting in startling comparisons for serious and comic effect with more confidence than she had shown in her previous work. The display of her genius for metaphor is not merely indulgence but rather a means of emphasizing the novel's broader themes. For example, Mr Tulliver provides his wife with an illustrative metaphor for her tendency to be prevented from acting by trivial obstacles: "You'd want me not to hire a good waggoner, cause he'd got a mole on his face" (*Mill*, I:2). When Mrs Tulliver insists that she never judged a man by a mole on his face, he protests: "No, no, Bessy; I didn't mean justly the mole; I meant it to stand for summat else" (*Mill*, I:2). Just as this basic if untutored capacity for comprehending the symbolic meaning of language distinguishes Mr Tulliver from his wife, so it divides Maggie and Tom. When Tom corrects her translation of a Latin word, she defends herself: "It may mean several things – almost every word does" (*Mill*, II:1). Maggie's imaginative, expansive nature comes into conflict with Tom's narrow, literal interpretation of familial duties and societal rule, comprising the basis of the novel's tragedy. In this light, what seems to be a passing reference to Aristotle is actually an expression of how fundamental the concept of metaphor is to the novel's development of character. It also hints at Eliot's desire to situate herself and her work in the tradition of great literature.

Although Eliot argued for the importance of her chosen genre of the realist novel as a modern equivalent to classical tragedy, she was strongly influenced by Aristotle's claim that tragedies, followed by epic poems, were the highest form to which an author could aspire. Her one epic poem, *The Spanish Gypsy*, was originally conceived as a drama. Though she never completed a tragedy, she studied the classical Greek dramatists intensively. She admired Sophocles (c. 496–406 BCE), and his *Antigone* shaped her thinking about dramatic form and also about a woman's conflicts between familial duty and citizenship, as she makes clear in her essay on "The *Antigone* and Its Moral" (1856): "Wherever the strength of man's intellect, or moral sense, or affection brings him into opposition with the rules which society has sanctioned, *there* is renewed the conflict between Antigone and Creon" (*SCW*, p. 246). She quotes from Sophocles' *Philoctetes* in "Amos Barton" and that tragedy of "a man who had a very bad wound in his foot" (*Mill*, II:5) resonates with both the name and the disability of Philip Wakem, who tells the story to Tom in *The Mill*. She also admired Euripides (c. 485–406 BCE) and identifies more with his plays than Sophocles' in her own aesthetic project since, according to Aristotle, Sophocles said that "he drew men as they ought to be, and Euripides as they were" (*Poetics*, 25), a distinction she echoes in her essay reviewing the works of the German socio-anthropological writer Wilhelm Heinrich von Riehl, "The Natural History of German Life": "The thing for mankind to know is, not what are the motives and influences which the moralist thinks *ought* to act on the laborer or the artisan, but what are the motives and influences that *do* act on him" (*SCW*, p. 264).

Portraying men as they were rather than as they ought to be was central to her fiction, and this brand of realism goes back to Euripides and also to Aristotle's pupil, Theophrastus (c. 372–287 BCE), who initiated a tradition of character writing that provided a classical model for her creations of realistic characters. She first read Theophrastus's *Characters* in Isaac Casaubon's Latin translation while living in Geneva. She returned to Theophrastus in her last work, *Impressions of Theophrastus Such*, which meditates on the question of literary influence, borrowing, and even plagiarism. The book gives us some insight into how conscious she was of the influence of past works on her own writing and of literary traditions constituted by acknowledged and unacknowledged influences: "Surely the acknowledgment of a mental debt which will not be immediately detected, and may never be asserted, is a case to which the traditional susceptibility to 'debts of honour' would be suitably transferred" (*TS*, 11). She believed in intellectual property rights, yet she also believed in influence and tradition. Writing to Alexander Main in 1873, Eliot emphasized that "when the consciousness is very full of a particular writer's mode of thought, it is almost a part of rectitude to avow the influence" (*GEL* V:404). Theophrastus learned from Aristotle, and writers for centuries have learned and borrowed from the *Characters*, as Eliot borrows the format and even the name of the ancient writer to weave modern character sketches into what Theophrastus calls the "backward tapestry of the world's history" (*TS*, 11).

The Bible formed a prominent part of Eliot's religious and literary inheritance. From her days of evangelical fervor through the end of her life, she made serious study of both the Hebrew Bible and the New Testament. Biblical references and allusions fill her letters and works. The biblical discourse of her most religious characters displays her remarkable knowledge of Scripture, her appreciation of the language of the sermon, and her awareness of the multiplicity of possible interpretations of the Bible. Three characters with radically different creeds and beliefs stand out: the Methodist preacher Dinah Morris in *Adam Bede*, the fifteenth-century Dominican monk Savonarola in *Romola*, and the Jewish visionary Mordecai in *Daniel Deronda*.

In addition to its pleas for sympathy with the common, working people of rural England, *Adam Bede* defends the Methodists against a presumed prejudice on the part of its readers. Methodists "sought for Divine guidance by opening the Bible at hazard; having a literal way of interpreting the Scriptures, which is not at all sanctioned by approved commentators" (*AB*, I:2). The conversation of the Methodists Dinah Morris and Seth Bede is punctuated with biblical quotations and Dinah makes her personal decisions based on this practice of bibliomancy.

Preaching on the Green in Hayslope, Dinah translates her biblical knowledge into the simple language of her audience and reflects on the power of the Gospels:

> "Dear friends," she began, raising her voice a little, "you have all of you been to church, and I think you must have heard the clergyman read these words: 'The spirit of the Lord is upon me, because he hath anointed me to preach the gospel to the poor.' Jesus Christ spoke those words – he said he came *to preach the Gospel to the poor*. I don't know whether you ever thought about those words much; but I will tell you when I first remember hearing them." (*AB*, I:2)

Describing her meeting with John Wesley, founder of Methodism, and her waking visions of the Passion, Dinah speaks "directly from her own emotions, and under the influence of her own simple faith" (*AB*, I:2). Her sermon is an inspired piece of writing on Eliot's part, juxtaposing biblical quotations with vivid images of Jesus on the cross. The simplicity of Dinah's faith and language, so effectively realized, should not prevent us from recognizing the profound knowledge of the text that Eliot displayed in writing such a scene and in her splicing quotations into the common dialect of other characters.

Dinah's sermon moves her listeners to repentance, even if only temporarily, as in the case of "Chad's Bess," who "wrenching her earrings from her ears, [she] threw them down before her, sobbing aloud" (*AB*, I:2). Similarly, in *Romola* the thunderous voice of Fra Savonarola preaching in the Duomo of Florence penetrates the minds and bodies of his hearers. The bewildered Baldassarre is unwittingly affected: "A voice that penetrated his very marrow with its accent of triumphant certitude was saying – 'The day of vengeance is at hand'" (*R*, II:24). His conversion is to an ethos of vengeance rather than repentance, but the effect of the preacher on the listener is equally powerful.

In his sermon, Savonarola, like Dinah, explains the path by which he became a spokesman for God:

> "And forasmuch as it is written that God will do nothing but he revealeth it to his servants the prophets, he has chosen me his unworthy servant, and made his purpose present to my soul in the living word of the Scriptures; and by the ministry of angels he has revealed it to me in visions."   (*R*, I:24)

Romola is layered with biblical language and imagery that combine Eliot's knowledge of scripture with her exhaustive study of the novel's Renaissance Florentine context. Like Dinah's sermons, those of Savonarola display both Eliot's facility in quoting biblical texts and her awareness of the power of the Word to transform hearers as well as readers.

Dinah's appropriation of biblical language to simple, accessible speech is intended to communicate to the greatest number, drawing simple lessons from the New Testament that were themselves addressed to the masses. Like Dinah and Savonarola, Mordecai (Ezra) Cohen is a visionary, but rather than reaching the many, his biblically-laced speech is poured into the ears of those closest to him and especially to his willing convert, Daniel Deronda. This contrast is important for two reasons. It shows the difference between Christianity – a proselytizing, populist religion – and Judaism, a non-proselytizing, exclusive religion. Secondly, this shift in the nature of visionaries from the first to the last of her novels reflects Eliot's changing artistic aspirations. She went from wanting to communicate to the many (and did so with the best-selling *Adam Bede*) to caring more about reaching the educated few, as is evident in the baffled reviews of *Daniel Deronda* that lamented her intellectual, esoteric dwelling on Judaism in comparison with the accessibility of her earlier novels.

Mordecai's language shows that the Torah, the Talmud, the Hebrew liturgy and Hebrew poetry (all of which Eliot studied in preparation for writing *Deronda*) are intermingled in his vision. When Daniel tells him, "We shall not be separated by life or death," his answer "was uttered in Hebrew, and in no more than a loud whisper. It was in the liturgical words which express the religious bond: 'Our God, and the God of our Fathers'" (*DD*, VIII:63). Before Ezra dies, he "uttered in Hebrew the confession of the divine Unity, which for long generations has been on the lips of the dying Israelite" (*DD*, VIII:70). This utterance signifies the passing of the soul of the tradition from Ezra to Daniel and Mirah. The power of such inheritance – through ritual and texts, whether Jewish or English Christian – preoccupied Eliot toward the end of her life as she thought about the future of England and about her own legacy. Her concern with literary traditions and the transmission of texts can shed light on our discussion of influences. What Eliot represents Mordecai as doing – transmitting a tradition – she simultaneously does herself. She chose, not the Shemah of Jewish tradition, but lines from John Milton's *Samson Agonistes* as the epilogue for *Deronda*,

> Nothing is here for tears, nothing to wail
> Or knock the breast; no weakness, no contempt,
> Dispraise, or blame; nothing but well and fair,
> And what may quiet us in a death so noble.

She chose to end her last novel with words from a great epic by a seventeenth-century English Christian on a subject taken from the Hebrew Bible and expressing a universalized sentiment on the common human experience of death.

As we are beginning to see, Eliot's novels are archives of textual quotations and allusions and are models of how to absorb, transform, and transmit inherited texts. Inevitably, Eliot was a devoted reader of England's greatest dramatist and poet, William Shakespeare (1564–1616). She and Lewes, who had a history as a theatre critic and actor and had played Shylock in regional theatre productions, read Shakespeare to each other (*GEL*, III:228–9) and saw numerous productions of his plays together. She learned from every aspect of his work, including his sonnets, on which she based her own "Brother and Sister" sonnets (1874).

Starting with *Felix Holt*, Eliot began providing epigraphs or mottoes for each of the chapters in her novels. Some she composed herself; others were drawn from a wide range of texts that reflect her vast reading. The mottoes are an indication of works that influenced her and also provide keys to the interpretation of her work, as the quoted text resonates with the situations and themes of the chapter it introduces. In *Felix Holt*, for example, 14 of 54 mottoes are from Shakespeare.[3] The general political theme and especially the relationship between the governors and the governed, the elite few and the masses, is enhanced through references to *Coriolanus*, which also reflect on Felix's character (*FH*, II:27, 30). Other Shakespearean histories, including *Richard II*, *Henry V*, and *King John*, further emphasize the themes in Eliot's "political novel."

In addition to her use of epigraphs, Eliot complicated the presentation of her characters by making analogies to Shakespearean characters, such as Mr Tulliver's Hotspur temperament, an allusion to *Henry IV* (Part I), a play that is also present in *The Mill* through the politics of water that ultimately prove "too many" for Mr Tulliver.

In *Daniel Deronda*, the narrator qualifies and adapts Shakespeare: "For Macbeth's rhetoric about the impossibility of being many opposite things in the same moment, referred to the clumsy necessities of action and not to the subtler possibilities of feeling" (*DD*, I:4). With the formal freedom to capture seeming paradoxes of human psychology, Eliot's narrator can observe: "We cannot speak a loyal word and be meanly silent, we cannot kill and not kill in the same moment; but a moment is room wide enough for the loyal and mean desire, for the outlash of a murderous thought and the sharp backward stroke of repentance" (*DD*, I:4). Much as she admired Shakespeare's plays, Eliot believed that her fiction could do more to represent realistic psychology.

Shakespeare pervades her work in ways that have been well studied. One of the lesser-explored aspects of Eliot's reading is that of the eighteenth-century poets, essayists and novelists. Her novels were made possible by the experimental fictions of her eighteenth-century predecessors, including Daniel Defoe, Samuel Richardson, and Henry Fielding, and she was aware of the debt she owed them.[4] Defoe (1660–1731) was well known to her, as the role of his *The Political History of the Devil* (1726) in *The Mill* suggests. A revealing if comic reference to his realism appears in "Brother Jacob" when pretty Penny Palfrey is impressed by David Freely: "A man who has been to the Indies, and knew the sea so well, seemed to her a sort of public character, almost like Robinson Crusoe or Captain Cook" (BJ, 2). That Penny does not distinguish between the fictional Crusoe and the historical Cook emphasizes the story's theme of the dangers of unrealistic literature.

In *Middlemarch*, she emphatically distinguishes her modern style of history writing from that of Henry Fielding (1707–1754) in the *History of Tom Jones* (1749). This "great historian, as he insisted on calling himself," enjoyed the leisure, the authority, and the absence of exacting standards – of both the novel as an art form and of knowledge generally – to digress and expound "over that tempting range of relevancies called the universe" (*MM*, II:15). Implied is a contrast of generations between Fielding and Eliot and also within the novel between Casaubon, whose "Key to All Mythologies" would explain everything, and Lydgate, whose ambition as a young pathologist is closer to Eliot's self-appointed job of "unraveling certain human lots, and seeing how they were woven and interwoven" (*MM*, II:15).

All of Eliot's novels are historical novels, recreating an historical past from a self-consciously modern perspective. The role of historian was one she took seriously, as her meticulous historical research for her novels suggests. She was impressed by her reading of the great historical novelist, Sir Walter Scott (1771–1832). Scott's fiction and poetry helped define her parents' generation, which provided the setting for *Scenes of Clerical Life, Adam Bede, The Mill, Felix Holt* and *Middlemarch.* She identified Scott, whom she had read aloud to her father, as an influence in shaking her from her orthodox views (*Haight,* p. 39). Following the success of *Adam Bede,* Lewes gave her a 48-volume set of Scott's novels, inscribing on the fly-leaf of the first volume that he was presenting her with the works of "her longest-venerated and best-loved Romanticist" (*GEL,* III:240). Her decision to write *Romola,* a novel further removed from her own place and time than any other she attempted, followed from this immersion in Scott's historical fiction, however different her representation of Renaissance Florence may seem from his depictions of the Scottish Highlands.

The British Romantic period of the late eighteenth and early nineteenth centuries was dominated by two very different novelists, Scott and Jane Austen (1775–1817), both of whom were important to Eliot. With Lewes, who was a great champion of Austen during a period when her novels were not as well remembered and respected as they later became, Eliot read all of Austen's novels. Austen's realism and subtle delineation of the complex relationship between characters informed Eliot's domestic satire, and some scenes in particular seem indebted to her novels. The presentation of the *tableau vivant* from Shakespeare's *The Winter's Tale* by Gwendolen, Rex and their friends in *Daniel Deronda* recalls the staging of *Lover's Vows* by the young people in *Mansfield Park.* Like Fanny's uncle, Sir Thomas, Gwendolen's uncle, the Revd Gascoigne, prohibits "the acting of scenes from plays" in his house. The novels' scenes are similarly fraught with undercurrents of sexual attraction (of Edmund for Mary Crawford and of Rex for Gwendolen). Both have the energy and excitement of young people at play; both are interrupted dramatically and come to an anti-climactic and thematically significant end with the return of the patriarch Sir Thomas and with Revd Gascoigne authoritatively locking the panel that has flown open to traumatize Gwendolen.[5] Additionally, when Stephen goes to find Maggie at her Aunt Moss's house in *The Mill,* the incongruity of his person with the surroundings, and the purpose of his visit – to woo an unwilling woman – recall Henry Crawford's trip to Fanny Price's home in Portsmouth to try to win her favor in *Mansfield Park.*

Eliot was an avid reader of Romantic poetry. Her debt to Wordsworth is particularly strong. The epigraph to *Adam Bede* is from Wordsworth's *The Excursion* (1814). In that novel Arthur Donnithorne mentions reading *Lyrical*

Ballads in which he is much struck by "The Rime of the Ancient Mariner" (*AB*, I:5). The supernatural nature of Coleridge's poem seems to resonate with the characters' superstitions in the novel, such as Adam's hearing the willow wand at his door on the night of his father's death and Elizabeth Bede's belief that "the dead are conscious" (*AB*, I:10). Arthur fantasizes that he might marry Hetty and about how "the men who come to the wedding breakfast" would envy her "hanging on his arm in her white lace and orange blossoms" (*AB*, I:15), suggesting the wedding feast in "The Rime of the Ancient Mariner," and in the novel's denouement, Hetty tells Dinah that she hated her baby, which seemed like "a heavy weight hanging round my neck," reminiscent of the Ancient Mariner's albatross. (*AB*, V:45).

Coleridge supplied supernatural poems for the *Lyrical Ballads*, but the fundamental aesthetic principles informing Eliot's writing have their origin in precisely those observations in Wordsworth's "Preface" to the *Lyrical Ballads* (1801) that are at odds with the supernatural and argue instead for the necessity of using "the very language of men" with "little falsehood of description."[6] *The Mill on the Floss*'s vision of childhood is in dialogue with Wordsworth's meditations on memory in poems such as "Tintern Abbey" (1798) and the "Intimations Ode" (1807). The epigraph to *Silas Marner*, from Wordsworth's "Michael" (1801) further confirms this influence.

The "second generation" Romantics were also important to Eliot, if less profoundly influential than Wordsworth. Mr Brooke (who has allegedly met Wordsworth), associates Will Ladislaw's romantic notions about art and social reform with Shelley. Ladislaw has also been connected to Lewes, whose youthful enthusiasm for Shelley took the form of his (unfulfilled) intention to write the poet's biography. In *Felix Holt*, Esther reads Byron and Felix prudishly objects: "His corsairs and renegades, his Alps and Manfreds, are the most paltry puppets that ever pulled the strings of lust and pride" (*FH*, I:5). Felix's objection is moral rather than aesthetic but it is clear elsewhere, for example in "Brother Jacob," that Byron's very unreality has a way of corrupting readers like Mrs Steene, who develops a "distaste for domestic occupations" after reading Byron's *Oriental Tales* (BJ, 2).

As for European Romanticism, Eliot was thoroughly familiar with the writing of Goethe. When she accompanied Lewes to Germany in 1854, it was to aid in his research for his English biography of the German Romanticist and she read most of his works during their nine-month stay. Her defense of Goethe appears in the essay, "The Morality of Wilhelm Meister" (1855). It was no wonder that Lewes was attracted to the poet, novelist and man of science, and this combination of qualities appealed to Eliot both in her husband and in Goethe.

Perhaps her favorite French writer was Jean Jacques Rousseau (1712–1778), of whom she said that it was worth learning French just to read his *Confessions* (*GEL*, I:xv). Her explicit homage comes in "The Lifted Veil" when Latimer, living in Geneva, "used to do as Jean Jacques did – lie down in my boat and let it slide where it would" (LV, 1) and in Theophrastus's reference to the *Confessions* as a model for autobiographical writing: "I too may be so far like Jean Jacques as to communicate more than I am aware of" (*TS*, 1).

Given Eliot's engagement with classic works of literature in all languages, and her preoccupation with recreating the social milieu of the generation preceding her own, the question of the extent to which she was influenced by her contemporaries is an intriguing one. Her stated aesthetic project is defined explicitly against the writing of her own age, as she makes clear in "Silly Novels by Lady Novelists" (1856) and other essays prior to her embarking on fiction. What she claimed to achieve – and in fact did – with her particular mode of realist representation was something many of her fellow Victorian realists were also claiming to have achieved. She enjoyed friendships and correspondences with the major novelists of her time, including Dickens, Thackeray, Trollope, and Gaskell, but she strove to distinguish herself from these contemporaries, all of whom were established novelists when she began to write fiction.

Before Eliot published her first works of fiction, Dickens had argued for the importance of representing the criminal classes (*Oliver Twist*, 1838). Gaskell made the case for representing the little-known working class in the Northern industrial city of Manchester (*Mary Barton*, 1848), and Trollope had represented in detail the provincial clergy in *The Warden* (1855) and *Barchester Towers* (1857). Eliot's plea for the importance of representing the peasant classes and for realistic representations generally must be read in the context of what these other novelists had achieved.

Her intention to separate herself from her contemporaries began before she started writing fiction. In "The Natural History of German Life," she refers to Dickens's *Little Dorrit* (1855–7), praising its realism but objecting to its lack of psychological depth. Although once established in her writing career she claimed not to read much contemporary fiction, she was part of the general movement toward realism in the Victorian novel.

Eliot was also familiar with the work of her contemporaries outside of England. Though Balzac was slow to be translated into English, Eliot was aware of his aesthetic determination to show what was "real." She marveled at Balzac's accomplishments but was put off by his rough and sexually explicit representations of Parisian life. Gwendolen's striking success and loss at the roulette table in the opening scene of *Daniel Deronda* evokes Eugene Rastignac's foray into gambling and dramatic success at the roulette table in *Père Goriot* (1835), with its emphasis on his role as the center of attention "with the eyes of all the spectators on him" (Ch. 2).

Eliot was ambivalent about all things American, but she admired some American writers. The "fall" of Hetty (Hester) Sorrell in *Adam Bede* recalls the fate of the fallen Hester Prynne in Hawthorne's *The Scarlet Letter* (1850). Eliot never met but corresponded with Harriet Beecher Stowe (1811–1896). Her review of Stowe's anti-slavery novel *Dred, A Tale of the Great Dismal Swamp* (1856) and her approving reference to Stowe in "Silly Novels by Lady Novelists" show her admiration for the American writer. *Daniel Deronda* was written after she began her correspondence with Stowe, and its ending, with Daniel leaving for the East to begin working toward a Jewish nation recalls the ending of *Uncle Tom's Cabin* (1852), in which the protagonist George Harris departs for Liberia to pioneer a new African nation of former slaves.

Eliot took at least some inspiration from the poets of her own age. She knew and admired Alfred, Lord Tennyson (1809–1892), and continued to read his work until the end of her life. She also read and respected both Robert Browning and Elizabeth Barrett Browning and corresponded with them, though it is difficult to detect any direct influence of these contemporary poets on her own poetry.

In considering the question of literary influences on Eliot, we must ask, as Eliot did in *Impressions of Theophrastus Such*: what is influence, as opposed to borrowing, responding, even plagiarizing? A catalogue of Eliot's references and allusions, together with evidence of less explicitly acknowledged influences would fill a book in its own right. While she strove to distinguish her unique and original artistic vision, Eliot's lifetime of intensive reading and engagement with the ideas of others inspired her to recognize the accomplishments of past writers, as well as those of her contemporaries.

Chapter 4

Works

Reviews and essays

Even in her early letters, it is evident that Mary Anne Evans was a natural born critic. She read constantly and extensively and wrote to share her opinions about what she read with friends, as when she observed that L. Vernon Harcourt's *Doctrine of the Deluge* – one of many attempts to uphold the veracity of the biblical flood in the face of geographical evidence refuting it – seemed to "shake a weak position by weak arguments" (*GEL*, I:34). In these letters, she exercised her critical mind even more than her creative imagination, and it seemed inevitable that when she considered a career, she thought of participating in the lively literary and intellectual exchanges taking place in the thriving Victorian periodical press.

In the review essays that Marian Evans wrote for various periodicals between 1849 and 1856, we can follow several strands of thought that help us to understand why she began to write fiction and also how she thought fiction ought to be written. Her journalism was the training ground for the penetrating analysis of her narrators. Her reviews and essays are important because they display the impressive range of her reading and knowledge by the time she was in her thirties, and because in them she works out some of the ideas about realist representation that she would later practice. She measured the writing of others according to a standard of "truth" and argued passionately for the moral necessity of such truth. In her ideas about the moral value of art, we can detect her earlier, religiously inspired desire to live in accordance with a high moral standard.

These reviews and essays were published anonymously in periodicals beginning with the *Coventry Herald and Observer* and including the *Westminster Review*, *Fraser's Magazine*, the *Saturday Review* and the *Leader*. After Eliot's death, Charles Lewes edited *Essays and Leaves from a Notebook* (1884). Thomas Pinney produced the first modern critical edition, the *Essays of George Eliot* (1963). Selections have been published in A. S. Byatt and Nicholas Warren's *George Eliot: Selected Essays, Poems and Other Writings* (1990) and in Rosemary

Ashton's *George Eliot: Selected Critical Writings* (1992). Reading these annotated essays in retrospect helps us to see the development of her critical mind and the way in which this thinking prepared for her fiction.

Looking at the collected essays, it is particularly intriguing to see how Eliot was able to follow the common theme of truth across disciplines and genres: religion, music, visual art, natural science, social science, poetry and fiction. When she moved to London and began her career as a journalist and editor, religion and its critics had preoccupied her for many years. Moving away from her earlier Evangelical phase, she had already subjected Christian belief to scrutiny through her reading of works such as Hennel's *An Inquiry concerning the Origin of Christianity* and her translation of Strauss's *Life of Jesus*. She remained intensely interested in the intellectual movements that were exposing as untrue beliefs that had held together Christian religion and society for centuries. In "Evangelical Teaching: Dr. Cumming" (1855), she refers to the Evangelical Dr Cumming – "as everyone knows, a preacher of immense popularity" (*SCW*, p. 140) – as one of those who does not "search for facts, as such, but for facts that will bear out their doctrine": "It is easy to see that this mental habit blunts not only the perception of truth, but the sense of truthfulness, and that the man whose faith drives him into fallacies, treads close upon the precipice of falsehood" (*SCW*, p. 145). Falsehood in religious belief, intellectual reasoning and ultimately in fiction became the target of her harshest criticisms.

The scientific method and the belief in facts and evidence influenced her thinking about the natural world and human society. Already in the forefront of intellectual developments of her day as editor of the *Westminster Review*, she became attuned to developments in scientific thought through her relationships with Spencer and then Lewes. In scientific inquiry, she found a new justification and authority for her search for truth and disdain for falsehood. While visiting Ilfracombe with Lewes, who was collecting specimens for *Seaside Studies*, she read in preparation for essays such as "The Natural History of German Life," and she wrote her "Ilfracombe Journal," in which she recorded her growing desire to know the names of things and "to escape from all vagueness and inaccuracy into the daylight of distinct, vivid ideas": "The mere fact of naming an object tends to give definiteness to our conception of it – " (*SEPW*, pp. 228–9). Such desire for definiteness was influenced by Lewes's scientific observations and became essential to her representational practice.

Before moving to London, she had published several pieces in the *Coventry Herald and Observer*, including "Poetry and Prose, from the Notebook of an Eccentric" (1846–7), written in the voice of a fictional narrator, and a brief review of J. A. Froude's controversial novel, *The Nemesis of Faith* (1849); and a review of R. W. Mackay's *The Progress of the Intellect* (1851) for the *Westminster*

Review. In the latter she mostly praised the author's ambitious attempt to show that "divine revelation is not contained exclusively or pre-eminently in the facts and inspirations of any one age or nation, but is co-extensive with the history of human development . . ." (*SCW*, p. 21). In descriptions that seem to foreshadow the fruitless attempts of Mr Casaubon to write a "Key to All Mythologies," she refers to "the mass of allusions and particulars with which Mr. Mackay overlays, rather than illustrates, his more general passages" (*SCW*, p. 26). Most importantly, she stresses a need for the "expansion of one's being into the past" (*SCW*, p. 19), a concept that describes her own attempts to extend the imaginations and sympathies of her readers to a past generation.

Having immersed herself in Goethe's writing while assisting Lewes with his biography in Germany, she took on English critics who charged the German writer with immorality. In "The Morality of *Wilhelm Meister*" (1855) she argues that his "pictures are truthful" – rather than didactic or melodramatic – and offer a "true morality" that is inseparable from his realism (*SCW*, p. 131). Here, realistic forms of representation are equated with telling the truth and hence Goethe's truth-telling is a higher form of morality than what passes for morality in public discourse, that is, sexual propriety. Undoubtedly, her personal situation – seeing herself as married where others saw adultery – influenced this and later commentary on the same subject, as in *Theophrastus Such*'s "Moral Swindlers" (16).

"Worldliness and Other-Worldliness: The Poet Young" further addresses the fallacies of religious belief. In this substantial essay, she pillories Edward Young, author of *Night Thoughts* (1741–5), a work she had once admired and knew by heart. "His muse," she writes, "never stood face to face with a genuine, living human being" (*SEPW*, p. 176); the moral spirit of his poetry is "low and false" (*SEPW*, p. 185); and his is a mind "deficient in sympathetic emotion" (*SEPW*, p. 207). The sharpness and hostility of this review epitomizes her own complete disillusionment with Evangelical thought and provides a platform for condemning unrealistic literature generally.

In a review of Tennyson's *Maud* (1855), she criticizes the poem but emphasizes her admiration for his earlier poem, "In Memoriam" (1850), with its "sanctification of human love as religion" (*SCW*, p. 172). This sanctification was consistent with her intellectual position and personal feelings at this time. It was also consistent with ideas expressed by Feuerbach in her recent translation of *The Essence of Christianity* (1854), particularly his beliefs about marriage, which helped her to justify her decision to live with Lewes in a marriage outside the bounds of the law and religion: "That alone is a religious marriage, which is a true marriage, which corresponds to the essence of marriage – of love" (*SCE*, p. 70). The notion that poetry is the place to explore the highest ideals of love and duty, which might serve instead of religion, is born out in her own poetic experiments in the 1860s–70s.

Some of Eliot's most feminist statements appear in her 1855 review discussing the writings of the American journalist Margaret Fuller (1810–50) and the eighteenth-century writer Mary Wollstonecraft (1759–97). She shows her typical cautiousness about political reforms but clearly believes in women's potential to develop under the right conditions:

> Unfortunately, many over-zealous champions of women assert their actual equality with men – nay, even their moral superiority to men – as a ground for their release from oppressive laws and restrictions. They lose strength immensely by this false position. If it were true, then there would be a case in which slavery and ignorance nourished virtue, and so far we should have an argument for the continuance of bondage. But we want freedom and culture for woman, because subjection and ignorance have debased her, and with her, Man . . .   (*SCW*, pp. 185–6)

In "Woman in France: Madame de Sablé" (1854), she argues that the fact of women's "comparative physical weakness, which, however it may have been exaggerated by a vicious civilization, can never be cancelled." This softness "introduces a distinctively feminine condition into the wondrous chemistry of the affections and sentiments" (*SEPW*, p. 8). And in a comment that reflects on her future pseudonymous authorship, which had readers guessing as to the identity and gender of the author, she writes in a review of Ashford Owen's *A Lost Love* (1855): "The author is unquestionably a woman, and writes like one in the best sense, namely, by keeping to the delineation of what a woman's experience and observation bring within her special knowledge" (*SEPW*, p. 330). One has to wonder whether Eliot applied this standard to herself.

Her best known and most extensive examination of women's writing appears in the less than complimentarily titled "Silly Novels by Lady Novelists," a satirical, engaging essay in which she outlines the species that fall within the genus "Silly Novels by Lady Novelists": "the frothy, the prosy, the pious, or the pedantic" (*SCW*, p. 296). Offering examples of ridiculous and unrealistic writing and exercising her sharpest wit, she sets the stage for the fiction she would soon begin to write. She argues "the most mischievous form of feminine silliness is the literary form, because it tends to confirm the popular prejudice against the more solid education of women" (*SCW*, p. 311). She makes sure to praise some of her more serious contemporaries: Harriet Martineau, Currer Bell [Charlotte Brontë], and Mrs [Elizabeth] Gaskell (*SCW*, p. 319). And she asks "Why can we not have pictures of religious life among the industrial classes in England, as interesting as Mrs. [Harriet Beecher] Stowe's pictures of religious life among the negroes" (*SCW*, p. 315).

This admiration for Stowe recalls her review of the American author of *Uncle Tom's Cabin*'s second novel of slavery, *Dred* (1856). Here Eliot offers a similar view about the degradation of slaves that she had presented with respect to women's oppression, namely, that representing an oppressed class as superior was counter-productive to liberationist arguments, tending only to suggest that virtue rather than vice is cultivated under oppressive conditions. Having praised the "conflict of races" portrayed in the novel, its Hebraic Christianity, and general realism, she observes that by representing the moral superiority of her slaves, Stowe commits "argumentative suicide," losing thereby "the most terribly tragic element in the relation of the two races – the Nemesis lurking in the vices of the oppressed" (*SEPW*, p. 381). This belief that vices should be realistically represented in all groups, including women, slaves, proletarians, and peasants, is a mainstay of her moral beliefs and aesthetic practice.

The view that oppression degrades and that degradation should be represented realistically, is also expressed in the essay that most substantially and explicitly establishes her aesthetic positions, "The Natural History of German Life," a review of two works by the German social theorist, Wilhelm Heinrich von Riehl. Before addressing the specifics of Riehl's work, she argues against false representations of "opera peasants" and other idealized stereotypes, asserting: "But our social novels profess to represent the people as they are, and the unreality of their representations is a grave evil" (*SCW*, p. 263). Emphasizing the moral importance of realistic representation, she writes: "The greatest benefit we owe the artist, whether painter, poet, or novelist, is the extension of our sympathies" (*SCW*, p. 263), a point she would repeat in *Scenes of Clerical Life* and *Adam Bede*. In this essay, we can see the influence of the art critic John Ruskin, whose *Modern Painters*, Vol. III (1856), she had reviewed in the same year. In her praise of Reihl's sociological and anthropological study of German peasants, she makes the case for realism in art.

Within two months of the essay's publication in July 1856, she would begin her first fiction, "The Sad Fortunes of the Reverend Amos Barton." After this, with a few minor exceptions, such as the "Saccharissa" essays (1865), she gave up journalism completely. The only other review she published came mid-way through her fiction-writing career and gives us a glimpse of the mature intellect and style she would have shown had she continued to write critical essays.

To help launch the *Fortnightly Review*, which Lewes had agreed to edit, she contributed a review of William Lecky's *The History of the Rise and Influence of the Spirit of Rationalism* (1865), one of the many ambitious Victorian analyses of the history of science and culture written for a popular audience. And it is Eliot's comments on the hypothetical "general reader" that are particularly interesting for what they show us about her attitude toward the British public before embarking on her most ambitious and difficult fiction and poetry. In her characterizations of the reader, we see foreshadowings of later characters – *Middlemarch*'s Mr Brooke, for example, who never goes "too far" into anything: "the general reader of the present day does not exactly know what distance he goes; he only knows that he does not go 'too far'" (*SEPW*, p. 389). She continues:

> This modern type of the general reader may be known in conversation by the cordiality with which he assents to indistinct, blurred statements: say that black is black, he will shake his head and hardly think it; say that black is not very black, he will reply, 'Exactly.' (*SEPW*, p. 389)

The word, "exactly" is a favorite of *Middlemarch*'s Sir James Chettam, who annoys Dorothea by his agreement with whatever she says.

The distance Eliot had traveled in her ten years as a novelist is striking. Her condescension to the general reader in 1865 seems far from the pleas for sympathy with the common people she had articulated in early essays, as well as from the appeal that her best-selling early works had for general readers. It is also revealing as an exercise in sketching the characteristics of a "modern type." Her last book, *Impressions of Theophrastus Such*, takes the form of essays that do just this – sketch modern types – but in the voice of a character/author, thereby combining her skills as an essayist with the creation of characters she had practiced in her novels.

In a review of Robert Browning's *Men and Women* (1856), she refers to Aristotle's works as characterized by "a majestic obscurity which repels the ignorant," and she applies this characterization approvingly to Browning's poetry, which has a majestic obscurity, "which repels not only the ignorant but the idle" (*SCW*, p. 234). In *Theophrastus Such*, she practices a comparable difficult and demanding obscurity. The history of her fiction-writing career, as we will see in the following sections, is the history of her movement toward this position of a writer who aimed to communicate, not with the ignorant and idle, but with the educated and the diligent reader.

Scenes of Clerical Life

In her early fiction, Eliot was intent on holding fast to her roots – in her imagination – even while her actions severed her from the people and places constituting those roots. By 1856, her family and the Midlands landscape of her youth existed for her only in memory. Her writing became a bridge between her past and present – a way to communicate the common experiences of the type of people she had known in her youth to the type of people she met in her new life.

Scenes of Clerical Life was serialized anonymously in *Blackwood's Edinburgh Magazine* (January–November 1857) and was published in book form with the newly invented pseudonym "George Eliot" on the title page (January 1858). In the first scene, "The Sad Fortunes of the Reverend Amos Barton" (January–February 1857), the unnamed male narrator asserts his intention to make the reader feel for unexceptional, commonplace people. As a child he attended Shepperton Church twenty five years earlier when the story takes place, and he recounts his tale from memory in an urban, literate voice reminiscent of essays like "Silly Novels by Lady Novelists". He tells any reader who may be unsatisfied with the ordinary people and events in his story to look elsewhere: "I learn from the newspapers that many remarkable novels, full of striking situations, thrilling incidents, and eloquent writing, have appeared only within the last season" (*Scenes*, I:5). Unlike the essays, however, the subject matter of clerical life gave Eliot the opportunity to dramatize the high value she placed on the ability not only to represent but also to communicate with ordinary people.

It is difficult to call the provincial clergyman whose sad fortunes are told in "Amos Barton" a hero. He is not even a vicar but only a curate, the lowly order of cleric who did the vicar's work for minimal pay. In addition to his unexceptional appearance, bad grammar and want of tact, this "quintessential extract of mediocrity" fails in his dutiful attempts to enlighten his poorest parishioners from sheer inability to sympathize and communicate with them. Following a comical scene in the parish work house – in which Amos fails to bring his "geographical, chronological, exegetical mind" down to the level of the "pauper point of view, or no view" (*Scenes*, I:2) – the narrator tells us:

> Alas! A natural incapacity for teaching, finished by keeping 'terms' at Cambridge, where there are able mathematicians, and butter is sold by the yard, is not apparently the medium through which Christian doctrine will distil as welcome dew on withered souls.   (*Scenes*, I:2)

In other words, though no elevated thinker himself and not well-prepared by his education at Cambridge, Amos is incapable of relating to the poor souls he hopes to reach, and so is perpetually ineffectual and – to the extent that he recognizes his failure – doomed to professional frustration that can make him irritable with his family and hence even more difficult for readers to like.

Such emphasis on language, communication, and sympathy suggests parallels between what a good clergyman should do and what a successful author should do. The clergyman's role as communicator and teacher may have been part of his attraction for Eliot as a subject. The connection is given an ironic twist by the claims of the (failed) clergyman Liggins to have written *Scenes*.

Furthering the implied analogy between cleric and author, the narrator holds up a minor character as a model of a "true parish priest":

> Mr. Cleves has the wonderful art of preaching sermons which the wheelwright and the blacksmith can understand; not because he talks condescending twaddle, but because he can call a spade a spade, and knows how to disencumber ideas of their wordy frippery.   (*Scenes*, I:6)

To write realist fiction and to communicate to a wide audience was Eliot's intention so that praise for a man who can "disencumber ideas from wordy frippery" without being condescending sounds like a model of writing as well as delivering sermons. If such ideals apply to Eliot's own practice, so they may apply to Lewes, with whom she was now living and who encouraged her to write fiction. Already a gifted popularizer of difficult philosophical ideas in his *Biographical History of Philosophy* (1845–6; 1857), Lewes was at this time engaged in writing *Seaside Studies*, a work that aimed to make the latest discoveries in natural science accessible to average readers. *Scenes* and *Seaside Studies* were written at the same time and both were serialized in *Blackwood's*.[1]

Amos's flaws are redeemed in the eyes of his parishioners, and of readers, by his wife Milly, a model of "gentle womanhood" (*Scenes*, I:2), domestic economy, and maternity. Everyone loves Milly, and even the gossiping neighbors who find fault with Amos wonder at her ability to raise six children so respectably on a curate's salary. The complicated plot whereby Milly is burdened with the presence of a penniless *faux* Countess – who unthinkingly avails herself of Amos's naïve hospitality – culminates in Milly's Christ-like death during the birth of her seventh child, who dies along with her. Milly has been physically worn out by the demands of wifehood and motherhood and is appreciated fully by her husband only after her death. While almost melodramatic in its pathos, the ending of the story stresses the good that follows Milly's death as the community that had earlier sniped so heartlessly at Amos rouses itself to sympathy and practical help for the poor widower and his children in the face of his loss: "Amos failed to touch the spring of goodness by his sermons, but he touched it effectually by his sorrows; and there was now a real bond between him and his flock" (*Scenes*, I:10).

In "Amos Barton," the image of the well-liked clergyman is invoked through passing references to the Reverend Gilfil, vicar for the parishes of Shepperton and Knebley in the previous generation. This recollection looks forward to Eliot's second "scene," "Mr. Gilfil's Love Story" (March–June 1857), which travels back in time to tell the story of the man only briefly remembered in her first tale. In "Amos Barton," the narrator coyly gestures toward the link between the stories, remarking of Gilfil, "I must not speak of him, or I might be tempted to tell the story of his life, which had its little romance" (*Scenes*, I:1). The comment shows that Eliot had already mapped out the connections between her scenes when she began, and in her next story, she proceeds to tell the history withheld in the first.

In addition to expanding the picture of her fictional Shepperton parish and town of Milby (based on her childhood memories of Chilvers Coton and Nuneaton) to include all classes of their inhabitants, "Mr. Gilfil's Love Story" shows thematic continuity with "Amos Barton" by treating the relative effectiveness of clergymen as well as the theme of reform, including technological and architectural "improvements," about which the narrator remains skeptical. Amos advocates the rebuilding and modernizing of Shepperton Church, and in "Mr. Gilfil," Sir Christopher Cheverel undertakes extensive architectural alterations of his ancestral home, expending his fortune on renovations inspired by his travels in Europe, especially Italy. The portrayal of Cheverel Manor draws on her memory of the Newdigate family, her father's employer.

On the one hand, the narrator admires Sir Christopher's endeavors and their results:

> . . . in walking through those rooms, with their splendid ceilings and their meager furniture, which tell how all the spare money had been absorbed before personal comfort was thought of, I have felt that there dwelt in this old English baronet some of that sublime spirit which distinguishes art from luxury, and worships beauty apart from self-indulgence. (*Scenes*, 2:4)

On the other hand, the narrator's stance toward the notion of modern improvements in both "Amos Barton" – in which he recalls "with fond sadness Shepperton Church as it was in the old days" (*Scenes*, I:1) – and to some extent in "Mr. Gilfil" as well, seems influenced by Jane Austen's ironic consideration of the relationship between tradition and improvement in *Mansfield Park* (1813). In that novel, the young heir Mr. Rushworth is absorbed in making "improvements" to his ancestral home, which Fanny Price laments as a loss of tradition (Vol. III, Ch. 9).[2] The eccentricity of the master's notions in "Mr. Gilfil" is summed up in the housekeeper's reaction when she learns of them: "'Olterations!' exclaimed Mrs. Bellamy, in alarm. 'What olterations?'" (*Scenes*, II:4).

Gilfil's romance revolves around a story in which he is marginal. He illustrates the narrator's generalization that "we mortals are often little better than wood-ashes – there is small sign of the sap, and the leafy freshness, and the bursting buds that were once there" (*Scenes*, 2:1). He provides a frame for the narrative of the Cheverel family and the orphaned Italian girl they bring to England following a trip to Italy. Caterina occupies a position in the childless household between daughter, pet (Sir Christopher affectionately calls her "monkey"), and servant. Opening in 1788, the story flashes back to the adoption of the child Tina in Italy in 1773, then resumes the story of her passionate love for the young heir to the manor, Captain Whybrow, who has encouraged her affection but now plans to make a suitable marriage. The scenario anticipates *Adam Bede* and Arthur Donnithorne's dangerous trifling with a woman beneath his station. In a turn of sensational plotting, Whybrow dies before Caterina can kill him, and the broken young woman – desperately and unrequitedly loved by the young Gilfil – is eventually persuaded to marry him. In a story similar to that of Rufus Lyon's marriage to the "blind French Catholic" Annette Ledru in *Felix Holt*, Caterina is grateful and dutiful to her husband, but dies in childbirth not long after the marriage. Gilfil resigns himself to a solitary life as a clergyman. Concluding with the metaphor of a tree, the narrator compares the elderly vicar to a "whimsical misshapen trunk," a nature "crushed and maimed . . . just when it was expanding into plenteous beauty" (*Scenes*, II:Epilogue). At the story's end, the narrator brings us back to where he began – to the 1820s and Gilfil's old age – making this second story a prequel to the first and third.

The three scenes of clerical life are linked by time, place, and theme. Just as anonymity, and later a pseudonym, provided a cover for the female author, each scene features a clergyman who is in fact of secondary importance to the woman in the story. In "Amos" and "Gilfil," the men provide the titles, a strategic authorial decision which cleverly foregrounds them in stories which emphasize the background – the women and wives. The title characters, while important, function as decoys, initially distracting attention from the female suffering, which unifies the stories as completely as the clerical theme.

In "Janet's Repentance" (July–November 1857), at once the most subtle and powerful of the three scenes, the woman emerges into the title, though she remains a background figure in the public life of her husband, Robert Dempster. Dempster is a lawyer whose powers of communication are mean-spirited and persecuting rather than beneficial. Like subsequent lawyers in her fiction, such as Wakem in *The Mill on the Floss* and Jermyn in *Felix Holt*, his glibness of tongue is sinister.

"Janet's Repentance" examines theological and social strife in the town of Milby around the year 1829. The town has been content in its Anglicanism and tolerant of the minor Dissenting presence among the downtrodden loom-weavers and coal-miners until a particularly conspicuous preacher begins to attract attention. Making inroads among the town's female population, the

ᵈ Tryan represents the Evangelical movement within the Church of
ᵗᵉ becomes the object of opposition and even hatred among some
ᵐbers of Milby society, especially Dempster, whose excessive
ᵏed among men because of his intellectual acumen and legal
ᵥife provokes a mixture of sympathy and censure for her
ᵤᵢs habit and her own pathetic recourse to drink as an escape.
The story touches on broad issues arising from the social transformation of
provincial towns in the early decades of the nineteenth century. Down certain
streets in Milby the handlooms may be heard clicking incessantly and pale,
narrow-chested weavers – looking forward to the central character in *Silas
Marner* – seem pitiful reminders of a dying livelihood. The "dismal lanes" of
Paddiford, where Tryan lives in a chosen state of self-denial and over-work, offer
"rows of grimy houses, darkened with hand-looms," with black dust whirling in
the cold November wind (*Scenes*, III:11). Ignorant and easily led townspeople
gather to mock Tryan and burn his effigy in an ugly scene anticipating the mob
that rampages in *Felix Holt*.

The story is rich with observations about the relationship between poverty,
ignorance and the rise of Evangelicalism, but it is undoubtedly most memorable
for its representation of the abuse suffered by Dempster's wife Janet. In an
unforgettable and disturbing scene, she is cast into the night by her drunken
husband:

> . . . a tender woman thrust out from her husband's home in her thin
> night-dress, the harsh wind cutting her naked feet, and driving her long
> hair away from her half-clad bosom, where the poor heart is crushed
> with anguish and despair.   (*Scenes*, III:15)

Here as elsewhere in *Scenes*, the style may seem florid in the Dickensian tradition
we have come to associate with Victorian melodrama (the tender woman, the
poor crushed heart). Any yet, what makes the image effective then and now is
the realistic detail ("her thin night-dress," "her naked feet") and the unflinching
account of suffering. Like a drowning man, Janet sees her life flashing before her
eyes and relives her transformation from a young girl, to a bride, to "the wife,
beginning her initiation into sorrow" to "the poor bruised woman, seeking
through weary years the one refuge of despair, oblivion" (*Scenes*, III:15).

Driven on this night to find comfort in the bed of a neighbor woman, Janet
determines to leave her husband and is gradually drawn to Tryan, less for his
religious teachings than for his condition as a fellow-sinner and fellow-sufferer
at the hands of the same brutal man as herself. Through Tryan, she finds the
sympathy that gives a new purpose to her life, and she is redeemed as a woman
who combines forgiveness and duty by nursing first her husband in his *delirium*

tremens and then Tryan in his consumption. Evangelicalism – the seductions of which Eliot had experienced herself and towards which she could be harshly critical, as in the essay, "Evangelical Teaching: Dr. Cumming" (1855) – emerges as an evil preferable to the worldliness and even the complacent forms of religion that characterize the majority of these townspeople.

"Janet's Repentance" sheds a harsh light on what in "Amos Barton" was bathed in a soft glow – the abuse of women. The centrality of the clergymen in the scenes misled most readers to assume that a man had written them. And yet, taken together, they are strikingly feminist. The sufferings of three women provide the main unifying theme of the deceptively titled *Scenes of Clerical Life*. Milly is run into the ground by childbearing and childcare. Caterina is treated as a pet by the Cheverels and dies bearing the child of a husband who worships her but cannot make her happy. Janet's physical abuse is portrayed graphically. Unlike Milly and Caterina, however, the latter adopts rather than bears a child and survives, and her story ends in her repentance for her drinking and her inheritance of money that will allow her to raise her child.

John Blackwood objected to the subject matter of "Janet's Repentance," and his criticisms probably explain why Eliot gave up further additions to the series. But she would not give in to pressure, and the novel she undertook next would treat even bleaker and more disturbing themes relating to the mistreatment of women.

Adam Bede

When she began writing *Adam Bede* in October 1857, George Eliot was living with Lewes in Richmond, just south-west of London. Although her irregular relationship had isolated her from surviving family members, she nonetheless was drawing on family memories to write her first novel. The novel was to be set between 1799 and 1801, two decades before her birth, and the memories were not of her own experience but rather of stories told to her by an older generation of relatives.

After she had finished *Adam Bede*, she recorded in a journal entry of 30 November 1858 how she had composed it. The "germ" of the novel was a story told to her by her "Aunt Samuel" (Elizabeth Evans, the wife of her father's younger brother, Samuel Evans) about a girl who was condemned to death for murdering her child. Aunt Samuel, a Methodist preacher, sat all night with the girl in her cell and rode with her in a cart to the gallows. This origin in an actual incident, together with the characterization of Adam based on aspects of her father's life, authenticates the novel's claim to truth. The realist principles she

articulated in "The Natural History of German Life" ar
Life are not only practiced in *Adam Bede*, but are st.
and explicitly in ways that established her as a spokes
realistic fiction.

In the novel's first sentence, she introduces a suggestive i.
mode of representation: "With a single drop of ink for a mi.
sorcerer undertakes to reveal to any chance comer far-reaching ν
past" (*AB*, I:1). Like the sorcerer, the novelist uses her ink to reveal ι.
to readers, but such writing is also a form of conjuring because one cannι.
hold a mirror to the people and events of the past. As the narrator explains
in a chapter entitled "In which the story pauses a little," she can only give "a
faithful account of men and things as they have mirrored themselves in my
mind" (*AB*, II:17). It is also in this chapter that she concentrates her arguments
for the ethical imperative of representing realistically "these more or less ugly,
stupid, inconsistent people, whose movements of goodness you should be able
to admire" (*AB*, II:17). Calling for sympathy with "common, coarse people,"
she argues: "It is so needful we should remember their existence, else we may
happen to leave them quite out of our religion and philosophy" (*AB*, II:17).

Unique to the chapter is another device designed to emphasize its realism:
the embodiment of the narrator as a person who knew and spoke to Adam
Bede in his old age. In what might seem to be a digression from the first
part of this pause, the unnamed narrator quotes the aged Adam's reflections on the Reverend Irwine and the man who succeeded him, "the zealous
Mr. Ryde," whose sermons were heavy on doctrine. These reflections, on a past
that comes long after the story told in the novel has ended, are presented before
the reader knows what the conclusion of that story will be and thus constitute
an odd, disjunctive moment in which the text looks forward in order to look
backward.

We do not know, for example, that Adam has been married to Dinah for
all these years, and that she would have had a great influence on his views
of religion. At the prodding of the narrator, Adam reveals that he preferred
the laid-back, non-doctrinaire Irwine to the more theoretical Ryde: "It isn't
notions sets people doing the right thing – it's feelings" (AB, II:17). In *Scenes
of Clerical Life*, the clergyman's ability to communicate with common people
is a metaphor for the novelist's ability to communicate. Eliot has the same
metaphor in mind when her narrator defends Adam against readers who "pant
after the ideal" (*AB*, II:17). Rather than panting after the ideal or propagating
notions, Eliot was striving in her fiction to set people "doing the right thing" by
emphasizing sympathy and feeling and by writing a novel that would impart
that message to as many readers as possible.

In *Adam Bede*, the image of the mirror is a complex metaphor for artistic creation and literary representation. It is also the means within the story – as it would be in subsequent novels – by which a character's narcissism is revealed. Hetty Sorrel performs her pigeon-like dance dressed in her makeshift finery before a mirror lighted with secreted candles. Later, Hetty looks into the dark pool when, in a blackened and inverted version of the Narcissus myth, she contemplates drowning herself.[3]

The novel asks us to consider Hetty simultaneously in relation to artifice and nature. The succession of metaphors employed to relate her story and foreshadow her fate are what make *Adam Bede* Eliot's most earthy and sexual novel. This frank sexuality receded in her work as she became more studied and intellectual in her approach to writing and as time distanced her from her country roots. Her first story, "Amos Barton," had at its center Milly Barton, who bore children until the bearing of a child killed her. After *Adam Bede*, we see just a few fertile women who seem inseparable from the breeding and milking that make up the rhythms of farm life. The farmer's wife Aunt Moss in *The Mill on the Floss* was described (until John Blackwood objected) as a "loosely-hung, child-producing woman" (*Mill*, I:8).[4] Tessa, *Romola*'s child-like Contadina, dwells among the farm animals in the countryside outside of Florence. Like Hetty, her soft, round prettiness leads to her seduction. After *Romola*, such images of natural maternity do not recur. The connections between human sexuality and nature that pervade *Adam Bede* reveal the provincial, rural sensibility – including its rhapsodies about the dairy and Hetty's round arms patting the butter – that clearly appealed to Eliot's primarily urban, middle-class readership.

Adam, hopelessly attracted to Hetty, opines that such attractions are mysteries like the "sprouting o' the seed" (*AB*, I:11). His acuteness with mathematics, as his mother notes, does not improve his ability to read character, and he is deceived by Hetty's "eyelids delicate as petals" and "long lashes curled like the stamen of a flower" (*AB*, I:15). The images are natural but they deceive Adam as to Hetty's lack of feelings. He imagines that she would "dote on her children," but the narrator undeceives the reader by noting the rather obvious fact that "there is no direct correlation between eyelashes and morals" (*AB*, I:15). The narrator tells us what Adam cannot know: Hetty dislikes the children for whom she cares and "would have been glad to hear that she should never see a child again" (*AB*, I:15). She is relieved when the "nasty little lambs. . . . *were* got rid of" (*AB*, I:15). She is not moved by the "downy chicks" and "would have hated the very word 'hatching,'" if she had not been bribed to attend them (*AB*, I:15). These images amount to heavy foreshadowing of Hetty's eventual detachment from her own child and her overwhelming desire to be rid of it.

Hetty's distance from lambing and hatching makes her seem unnatural; and yet, we cannot help but reflect that such instances of agricultural production represent the unnatural human manipulation of natural processes that constitutes farming. Furthermore, Nature provides its own examples of maternal rejection, as when Mrs Poyser tells her boys, who have found the speckled turkey's nest, not to frighten the mother, "else she'll forsake it" (*AB*, II:18). Hetty's very hardness, well concealed by her external softness and her general silence, is shown through natural metaphors. The narrator observes that "people who love downy peaches are apt not to think of the stone" (*AB*, I:15), while Mrs Poyser says of Hetty that she is "no better nor a cherry wi' a hard stone inside it" (*AB*, III:31). Peach and cherry stones, after all, are just as natural as downy things, though human beings prefer what is soft to what is hard in nature.

After Hetty is arrested for abandoning her baby, she tells Dinah that during her ordeal: "My heart went like a stone" (*AB*, V:45). After prompting her to confess, however, Dinah says that she is "no longer hard" (*AB*, V:45). Hetty's softening as a result of Dinah's religiously-infused love finds its parallel in Adam's experience, for he perceives his own moral failing to be hardness toward the weakness of others, and having suffered with Hetty through her ordeal, vows that he "will never be hard again" (*AB*, V:42). This resolve is repeated when Adam encounters Arthur after Hetty's transportation, and tells him that being hard is "in my nature" (*AB*, V:48). In going against his nature, and being softened, he is prepared to receive Dinah's love.

Hetty is almost too beautiful to be real. Her dressing up before the mirror and her ironic impersonation of Dinah create an *alter ego* to Hetty the peach and cherry. Mrs Poyser complains: "Anybody maight as well set a pictur to watch the children as you" (*AB*, II:18). The couple that meets Hetty briefly during her journey is struck with her beauty, and the husband remarks that she is like "a pictur in a shop-winder" (*AB*, V:36). The seeming contradictions in the metaphors of Hetty as at once natural and artificial may express Eliot's ambivalent judgment of her wayward egoist – a pitiful mother who forsakes her nest in fright and a literary character whose shocking actions test the reader's sympathies.

Morality in *Adam Bede* lies in the natural feeling of connection to place and in reverence for familial duty. The narrator remarks:

> There are some plants that have hardly any roots: you may tear them from their native nook of rock or wall, and just lay them over your ornamental flower-pot, and they blossom none the worse. Hetty could have cast all her past behind her and never cared to be reminded of it again.   (*AB*, I:15)

In contrast, Adam voices the author's preferred morality: "We can't be like the birds, as fly from their nest as soon they've got their wings, and never know their kin when they see 'em, and get a fresh lot every year" (*AB*, I:16). To be human, as the naturally moral Adam recognizes, is to be faithful to spouses and to recognize kin.

The childhood memories that bind Adam to his alcoholic father, together with his dutiful actions toward his mother and brother, confirm him as the novel's moral center. Adam is superior morally because he is bound to his place, his parents and his brother. And yet, a transplanted moral life is also possible. Some uprooted characters adapt to a new environment and thrive there. Dinah relocates to marry Adam, and Bartle Massey leaves his mysterious past behind and devotes himself to educating the young men of Hayslope. The tension between a morality based on connection to place and the possibility of remaking oneself in a new environment suggests Eliot's experience of abandoning the home of her childhood and then striving to revive and recreate it in memory for a moral purpose.

Questions about what is natural as opposed to what is human and social are evident in Eliot's belief that maternal qualities are not necessarily delimited by sex. While Hetty is neither happily domestic nor maternal, Bartle prides himself on his homemade bread and immaculate housekeeping. He is also, despite his hard talk, maternal in his caring for his dog Vixen and her pups and in his caring for Adam during Hetty's trial. Adam's softhearted, Methodist brother Seth tends the kitchen fire and prepares tea for his mother. The novel's final scene finds him playing happily with Adam's children. These bachelors prepare the way for Eliot's most extended treatment of male domesticity and maternal instincts in *Silas Marner*, the novel she would write following her sustained examination of the social construction of gender in *The Mill on the Floss*.

The Mill on the Floss

Adam Bede was the making of George Eliot. Its reviews were resoundingly positive and its sales were greater than either Blackwood or Eliot had imagined. Gordon Haight declares: "No book had made such an impression since *Uncle Tom's Cabin* swept the world."[5] Despite doubts that she would ever be able to write anything as good as *Adam Bede* again, Eliot turned her attention to her next novel, which was to draw on even more personal memories and experiences than the once-removed recollections of the previous generation.

In preparation for the new novel, she and Lewes scouted out scenes that would provide a basis for her descriptions of the fictional town of St. Ogg's and her fictional rivers, the Floss and its tributary, the Ripple. Though it drew on her childhood memories, the story was not to be set in the Midlands. On a visit to Weymouth on 5 September 1859, they toured a mill that helped fill in realistic detail for the mill she imagined, and in November they traveled to Gainsborough in Lincolnshire, where the town and its tidal river, the Trent, met her needs exactly. The novel was published in three volumes on 4 April 1860. Eliot received £2,000 for the first 4,000 copies, which quickly sold out. The reviews too were positive, and Eliot's reputation as the most formidable new voice in fiction was established.

The natural imagery and metaphors that Eliot used to characterize Hetty Sorrel and to foreshadow the death of her child in *Adam Bede* are expanded in *The Mill* and adhere particularly to Maggie Tulliver. Animal analogies abound. In the first chapter alone, the nine-year-old Maggie is compared to a Skye terrier, a long-tailed sheep, and a Shetland pony. Reflecting her parents' view that she is overly "cute" (acute) but will "fetch none the bigger price for that," and her father's puzzlement at the results of the "crossing o' the breeds" (the Tulliver and Dodson families), the narrator refers to her as a "mistake of nature" (*Mill*, I:1). Such language reveals Eliot's awareness of contemporary scientific writing. Darwin published *On the Origin of Species* in 1859 and Eliot read it after she had begun *The Mill*. While she was writing her novel, Lewes was researching his *Studies in Animal Life* (1862). *Adam Bede* showed Eliot's tendency to situate human lives in terms of the natural processes of reproduction; in *The Mill* her analysis of families and inherited traits is even more pronounced. The perceived unnaturalness of Maggie's intelligence and strong-willed personality – so bewildering to her simple-mindedly feminine mother – is further emphasized when the mill hand Luke consoles her for having forgotten to feed her brother's rabbits by insisting that the fancy, lop-eared breeds were not likely to survive anyway: "Things out o' natur niver thrive. God A'mighty doesn't like 'em" (*Mill*, I:4).

This observation together with Mrs Tulliver's anxiety about the river is ominous. Mrs Tulliver tells Maggie: "You'll tumble in and be drownded some day" (*Mill*, I:2). She later predicts that her children will be "brought in dead and drowned some day" (*Mill*, I:10). In this respect, Mrs Tulliver, so unperceptive in other aspects of life, serves as an oracle enhancing the tragic dimensions of the novel. Like the natural metaphors anticipating Hetty's child-murder in *Adam Bede*, these foreshadowings indicate that Eliot had her conclusion in mind from the start.

Watery deaths held a particular fascination for Eliot. In *Adam Bede,* Thias Bede falls into a stream and drowns. In *Romola,* Tito and Baldessarre struggle to their deaths after falling into the river Arno. In *Daniel Deronda,* Mirah tries to drown herself in the Thames and Grandcourt drowns in a boating accident on the Mediterranean Sea. Maggie is fascinated by an illustration in Daniel Defoe's *The Political History of the Devil,* in which a woman accused of being a witch is thrown into a pond. If she floats, she is a witch and must be killed; if she drowns, she is proved innocent by her death. Maggie knows instinctively that, metaphorically speaking, such is her own lot, and repeatedly, with respect to her brother Tom and her loyalty to her family, she finds that she stands to lose, whatever choices she may make. This is true in small incidents, as when Tom insists that she take the bigger portion of a jam puff she has fairly chosen, but berates her as greedy when she eats it without offering him some. And it is also true in the larger dilemma Maggie faces toward the end of the novel when she refuses to marry Stephen in favor of retaining ties to her family, only to be rejected by her brother for her disgraceful behavior with Stephen.

Thus there is an interesting sense in which water is associated with beginnings and endings: literally of origins and deaths, and metaphorically as the introduction and conclusion of the novel. The first chapter presents a first-person narrator watching a girl who is watching the river turn the mill. As he looks at the full river with its lush banks and bobbing ducks, he confesses, "I am in love with moistness . . ." (*Mill,* 1:1). From this point on, water imagery pervades the novel, with its myth of St. Ogg ferrying the Virgin across the Floss, Maggie's floating away with Stephen, and finally the flood that makes its climax. We soon learn that the narrator's vision was a dream recalling the girl Maggie whose image was conjured by his intention to tell us her story.

In "How I Came to Write Fiction" (1857), Eliot describes herself in a similar state while lying in bed thinking about the subject of her first story: " . . . my thoughts merged themselves into a dreamy doze, and I imagined myself writing a story of which the title was – 'The Sad Fortunes of the Reverend Amos Barton'" (*SCW,* p. 323). The dreamy doze is incorporated as the beginning of *The Mill* as it meditates on the profoundly unconscious origins of fiction.

Not surprisingly, Eliot's thinking about water is not merely the product of her observations of natural phenomena, but shows philosophical influences. Lewes's *Biographical History of Philosophy* begins with the Greek philosopher Thales, who asserted, "the principle of all things is water."[6] According to Lewes, his great contribution was the recognition that "[m]oisture was the Beginning" and is "the origin, the starting-point, the primary existence."[7] Beginning *The Mill* with the love of moistness and making water the starting point of memory – her own memory being the inspiration for the novel – was a way to introduce the philosophical concerns flowing through Eliot's most autobiographical novel.

The controlling images of water generally and the river in particular are simultaneously deathly and generative. The Floss flows eternally to the sea, and the mill that it turns represents the human attempt to harness the power of nature. The river functions like an angry god providing a *deus ex machina* to the novel's tragedy. At the same time the flood that provides its culmination is a natural phenomenon reminding us that rivers cannot be harnessed. Eliot combines images of the "deluge" in Genesis with her sophisticated knowledge of scientific research refuting the validity of the biblical account. The synthesis of myth and empirical science is one of the most remarkable characteristics of *The Mill*.

Mr Tulliver's lawsuits start the tragedy in motion. The narrator emphasizes his tragic condition: "Mr. Tulliver had a destiny as well as Oedipus" (*Mill*, I:13). The tragic elements of the novel were noticed by contemporary reviewer E. S. Dallas, who observed in a review for *The Times*: "The riddle of life as it is here expounded is more like a Greek tragedy than a modern novel."[8] But Tulliver's legal battles are situated firmly in early nineteenth-century questions of land and water usage. His first lawsuit involves the right of way over his property; the second is over a dam; the third is over irrigation technology, which he feels sure will violate his water rights. Tulliver believes that his neighbor's diversion of the river to irrigate his land will reduce the flow of water to turn his mill. It is unclear in the novel how far his suspicions are correct, but his "Hotspur" temperament, which, like the river, cannot be contained, leads him into a futile legal case, which results in his "fall" – literally from his horse – and figuratively from the socially respected and affluent miller to an ineffectual, emasculated near-bankrupt. He becomes as weak as his brother-in-law Moss, whose poverty he had disdained but to whom he had nonetheless given money in an act of generosity that would increase his own debt.

Following the narrator's reverie, the novel opens with Mr Tulliver brooding over his son Tom's education. He wants Tom to be something better than a miller, but also a son who will help him to negotiate the bewildering legal forest into which he has naively wandered. The way in which he talks about Tom as an instrument for achieving his own designs contributes to the sympathetic portrait of pressures facing sons whose fathers make decisions about their futures without consulting them. This sympathy mitigates the portrait of Tom as young tyrant, exercising a will, mostly over Maggie, which he has been raised to believe is predominant. It is clear that Eliot meant readers to sympathize with Tom, but the overall effect of the novel was perhaps beyond her artistic control, reflecting unconscious resentments she had about her brother Isaac's patriarchal attitude toward his younger sister.

Eliot's most autobiographical and Romantic novel, *The Mill* also recounts the inscription, through family influences and education, of gendered characteristics on young people, thus revealing her opinions and questions about the ways boys and girls are molded into conventional gender roles. This socialization reinforces natural tendencies, but not always for the best. In *George Eliot* (1902), Leslie Stephen, man of letters and father of Virginia Woolf, criticized the male characters in *The Mill*, arguing that Eliot was "too thoroughly feminine to be quite at home in the psychology of the male animal."[9] It is difficult, however, to reconcile this late Victorian's reading with Eliot's careful analysis of Tom's character and education.

Tom's native masculinity and lack of imagination are chronicled through a series of brilliantly realized scenes in the first two books of the novel. The supremacy he has enjoyed as the eldest son of a successful provincial miller is challenged when he is sent to study under a clerical tutor of limited intellectual capacities and with even greater limitations in his ability to consider the practical results of his tutoring. Tom is ashamed of his obtuseness in the study of Latin and Euclidian geometry, and he is reduced further by being asked to care for his tutor's daughter. This role in Mr Stelling's household makes him "more like a girl than he had ever been in his life before" (*Mill*, II:1) and was certainly not what his misguided father had in mind when sending him to receive a superior education.

Rather than softening Tom, however, these experiences seem to reinforce his desire to assert authority when he comes back into the orbit of his superiority at home. Perhaps the rawest expression of Tom's reactionary disdain for weakness and feminine expressions of imagination comes in his stamping on the earwig about which Maggie has spun a story to entertain their cousin Lucy: "Tom had a profound contempt for this nonsense of Maggie's, smashing the earwig at once as a superfluous yet easy means of proving the entire unreality of such a story" (*Mill*, I:10). One has to wonder whether Virginia Woolf was thinking of Tom Tulliver and her father's critique of him when she had Giles Oliver stamp on the abomination of a snake unable to swallow a frog in *Between the Acts* (1941). Both scenes powerfully illustrate an intolerant masculinity and show a female author's recognition of the male dominance Eliot portrayed. This connection is enforced by Tom's disgust at the unnatural relationship between the deformed Philip Wakem and his sister.

Maggie seeks acknowledgment and approval from men whose intelligence Eliot undercuts, including her father, Mr Riley, and Mr Stelling. Eliot herself was often bored with female company and clearly strove to impress men with her intellectual abilities, including her father, Charles Bray, John Chapman, and Herbert Spencer. Yet, her heroines are often misguided in the men from whom they seek affirmation. In *Middlemarch*, Dorothea wants to impress Mr Casaubon. In *Daniel Deronda*, Gwendolen takes pleasure in impressing her uncle and then, against her own rational judgment, strives to win the attentions of Grandcourt. She has a sense of herself as reflected in public opinion and specifically in the homage of men. She dismisses women generally, "and when left alone in their company had a sense of empty benches" (*DD*, II:11).

The biographical aspects of the sexual dynamics in *The Mill* are complicated. Maggie's rejection of Philip and his assumption that her feelings relate to his physical appearance and disability seem infused with Eliot's recollections of her own rejection by Chapman and Spencer, both of whom made it clear that her lack of physical beauty was the primary cause of their inability to find her sexually attractive. This leads us to believe that when Leslie Stephen commented on the femininity of her male characters, he was overlooking the way in which, for her, masculine and feminine characteristics are separate from sexuality. Tom's masculine actions, for example, do not translate into sexual potency. His sexuality is addressed only obliquely through his attraction to his cousin Lucy, to whom he had shown special attention in childhood, and to whom he gives a dog. His attraction to her is only suggested; but no other love interest enters Tom's life. This reveals something significant about Tom. Perhaps he is ground down by his duties and work, or perhaps, like Maggie, he cannot look beyond the family for his intimate ties. His asexuality as a young man seems to suggest regions Eliot could not explore further, and situates him within the tradition of other characters like Seth Bede and Silas Marner, rather than within the real family romance of her conventionally married brother Isaac.

As Eliot herself realized, the later books of *The Mill* are incompletely integrated with the early books. This shift begins in Book VI with a gap of time in which, following the financial ruin of her family and death of her father, Maggie has gone off to become a teacher and is returning to visit her cousin Lucy, now engaged to Stephen Guest, whose father owns the company for whom Tom now works. The principal characters are older, and an amnesia sets in about the events represented in the first five books – about Mr Tulliver's lawsuit, his quarrel with lawyer Wakem and Maggie's friendship with Philip. Mary Poovey has noted that "by the opening of the final book, all of the problems of what had previously constituted the novel's structural secret or ground – the financial plot – have been resolved, and the narrative result is that the financial plot ceases to have any importance at all."[10] To the characters, if not to the readers, the past now has a hazy insignificance. Lucy tells her fiancé Stephen, a character newly introduced to the novel: "There were painful circumstances, I believe. I never quite understood them, or knew them all" (*Mill*, V:1).

This absence of memory about the past is part of what tempts Maggie when she is faced with her attraction to Stephen and her struggle with Tom, who wants her to stop working and let him support her. Stephen is a privileged young man much like *Adam Bede*'s Arthur Donnithorne. His "attar of Roses" fragrance recalls the "rose scent" Hetty detects in Arthur's hair and suggests an egotistical, spoiled indulgence that marks a contrast with the hard life Maggie and Tom have had to pursue to support themselves.

Stephen comes into Maggie's life after her character is formed. He is distinguished from Tom, Lucy, and Philip by not having any claim on her earliest affections. This is intentional on Eliot's part and provides the primary basis of Maggie's conflict. He lacks that deep-rooted connection that we have to people we have known since childhood. For all her sexual attraction to Stephen and the seductiveness of his offer to marry her and take her away, she cannot forsake the ties that have formed her. In this, *The Mill* recalls Wordsworth's poetry, especially "Tintern Abbey" in which he shows that his relationship to his sister is more important than any other tie in his life.

The "root of piety" to which Maggie sacrifices her potential domestic and sexual happiness has made *The Mill on the Floss* a controversial novel. Unlike William and Dorothy Wordsworth, Maggie and Tom die in an expression of filial bonding and in a flood predicted from the start of the novel. Eliot drove her heroine into a hopeless corner and liberated her in death. The endings of her novels in the future would be less dramatic, but perhaps not less pessimistic. After *The Mill*, her fiction moved further and further from that strata of memory that she had mined in her early works. In keeping with its classically tragic associations, *The Mill* was cathartic for her. She could now move on to new and innovative fictional experiments, liberated from the burdens and demons of her past.

Silas Marner, "The Lifted Veil," and "Brother Jacob"

In November of 1860, George Eliot was enjoying the success of *The Mill on the Floss* and contemplating an historical novel set in Renaissance Florence. Before the novel that would become *Romola* had progressed very far, however, she was inspired with a new idea. She recorded in her journal that an English story had thrust itself between her and her Italian novel. The story would become *Silas Marner, the Weaver of Raveloe* (1861).

Silas Marner (1861) is unusual among Eliot's novels because, though realistic in external detail and psychological analysis, it is primarily a fable. It explores complex human relations, and yet its moral is straightforward: money is worthless compared to the love of another human being and the fellowship of community. The themes running through this story of a miser and the young girl he adopts may be highlighted by considering it in the context of two very different short works that she wrote at about the same time. "The Lifted Veil" (1859) and "Brother Jacob" (written in 1860, published in 1864), though less substantial, have many similarities with *Silas Marner* and like it served Eliot as artistic and emotional releases from the demands of writing her longer novels.[11]

"The Lifted Veil" and "Brother Jacob" express the dark side of what Eliot intended to be morally instructive fiction. The sarcastic narrator of "Brother Jacob" does not sympathize with the story's characters. The corrupt protagonist David Faux is unredeemable; the villagers are greedy, gullible fools. "The Lifted Veil" is unrelieved by humor and thus offers an even darker perspective on the notion of sympathy with others. In contrast, *Silas Marner* expresses the light side of the dark relationships Eliot would portray in *Romola*. Whereas in *Romola*, an adopted child abandons and denies his father, in *Silas Marner*, a child shows loyalty to her adopted father, preferring a simple life with him to a wealthier home with her belatedly revealed biological father. In these works Eliot's perceptions of, and opinions about, familial relations vacillate between extremes.

"The Lifted Veil"

"The Lifted Veil" thrust itself upon Eliot as she was beginning to write a more ambitious work, *The Mill on the Floss*. "The Lifted Veil" is Eliot's only supernatural story. Its strangeness and morbidity were noted by Blackwood, who agreed to publish it in *Blackwood's Magazine* (July 1859), perhaps to humor the newly successful author of *Adam Bede*. Eliot seems to have had some qualms about the story and added a healthily moral epigraph when it was republished in the 1878 Cabinet edition: "Give me no light, great Heaven, but such as turns / To energy of human fellowship. / No powers beyond the growing heritage / That makes completer manhood." The images of light, energy, and power anticipate Latimer's strange gifts in the story, but the epigraph rejects any powers that do not promote fellowship, heritage, and manhood. It prompts us to read the story as carrying a moral message but does not foreclose other interpretations.

Having asserted the importance of realism and of sympathy in her essays and fiction up to his time, Eliot momentarily reacted against the restraints of realism and even the efficacy of sympathy in this tale of a man who suffers from two super-human powers: the ability to "hear" the thoughts of others and the ability to foresee his own death. Both of these powers rob him of the ignorance that allows human beings to act morally and meaningfully. Because he hears the trivial thoughts of others (including their negative opinions about him), he cannot sympathize with them. Because he knows when and how he will die, he lacks that striving to make meaning of a life that is precious precisely because we do not know when it will end.

Among the visions that make up Latimer's intense mental life is that of a bridge in Prague, a city he has never visited. In his reverie he sees blackened statues lining the "unending" bridge and imagines them suffering from eternal life, "urged by no fear or hope, but compelled by their doom to be ever old and undying, to live on in the rigidity of habit, as they live on in perpetual mid-day, without the repose of night or the new birth of morning" (LV, Ch. 1). Such a hellish sentence recalls that endured by the Struldbruggs in Book III of Jonathan Swift's *Gulliver's Travels* (1726). What might seem like the realization of an eternal human wish to live forever is presented by Swift as "the dreadful prospect of never dying."[12] Knowing they will not die leads the decrepit Struld-bruggs to be not only "opinionative, peevish, covetous, morose, vain, talkative; but uncapable of friendship, and dead to all human affection".[13] Like the statues, Latimer has neither fear nor hope, two human qualities that depend on ignorance of the future. Like the Struldbruggs, Latimer can be peevish, morose and dead to human affection.

Latimer is associated not only with the Struldbruggs but, through his first-person narration and his misanthropy, with Swift's narrator, Lemuel Gulliver. In Swift's fantasy, Gulliver is a literal traveler, whereas Latimer is a virtual traveler of the mind. That Eliot was thinking of Swift is clear from Latimer's quotation of the Latin epigraph on Swift's tombstone: "*ubi soeva indignatio ulterius cor lacerare*" ("where savage indignation can no longer lacerate the heart"). While he awaits his foreseen death, Latimer writes bitterly of the sympathy bestowed upon the dead that was denied them in life: "It is only the story of my life that will perhaps win a little more sympathy from strangers when I am dead, than I ever believed it would obtain from my friends while I was living" (LV, Ch. 1). He views death as the only relief from the hypocrisy and cruelty of human society.

"The Lifted Veil" was Eliot's first experiment with an embodied first person narrator since "Poetry and Prose from the Notebook of an Eccentric," and her last until *Theophrastus Such*. Latimer, like Theophrastus, is a failed author and is certainly not Eliot, but his passive wish for the cessation of all noise is a sentiment similar to a desire she expressed in her darker moments, as in a letter to Cara Bray: "It must be easier to die for the world than to live for it – easier to die for a principle than to act up to it, and I should be quite glad of such a *short cut* to virtue" (*GEL*, I:190). Latimer refers to death as a blessed oblivion: "the eye will cease to entreat; the ear will be deaf; the brain will have ceased from all wants as from all work" (LV, Ch. I). He looks upon death as a release from the incessant noise around him created by the consciousnesses of others.

Hearing as a metaphor for sympathy has an interesting evolution in Eliot's work. The narrator in "Janet's Repentance" states earnestly:

> Yet surely, surely the only true knowledge of our fellow-man is that which enables us to feel with him – which gives us a fine ear for the heart-pulses that are beating under the mere clothes of circumstance and opinion. (*Scenes*, III:10)

In "The Lifted Veil," too much knowledge is maddening, "like a preternaturally heightened sense of hearing, making audible to one a roar of sound where others find perfect stillness" (LV, 1). In *Middlemarch*, the preternatural ability to hear is associated with death: "If we had a keen vision and a feeling for all ordinary human life, it would be like hearing the grass grow and the squirrel's heart beat, and we should die of that roar which lies on the other side of silence" (*MM*, II:20). By the time she wrote *Middlemarch*, she considered deafness to sounds, which in "Janet's Repentance" promised sympathy, to be a precondition for living.

"The other side of silence" in *Middlemarch* presents an image similar to that of "the lifted veil." "The Lifted Veil" ends in a scientific experiment when Mrs Archer, a household servant who has died and been brought back to life by a blood transfusion, accuses Latimer's wife Bertha of plotting to kill him.[14] When the veil is lifted, it reveals knowledge taken to the grave and unnaturally recovered. It is an ugly knowledge – perhaps better left veiled – just as people, according the narrator of *Middlemarch*, are better off for being "well wadded in stupidity" (II:20).

"Brother Jacob"

After portraying the positive brotherhood between Adam and Seth in *Adam Bede*, Eliot explored the mixed nature of sibling relations in *The Mill on the Floss*. "The Lifted Veil," "Brother Jacob" and *Silas Marner* all reflect negatively on the relationship between brothers. Latimer covets his brother's fiancée Bertha and marries her after his brother dies in an accident. "Brother Jacob" gives a darkly comic spin to Maggie's binding fidelity to Tom in *The Mill* when David Faux cannot rid himself of Jacob, his blundering idiot brother who epitomizes appetite and parodies filial affection. *Silas Marner* pits the selfish, blackmailing Dunsey Cass against his brother Godfrey, made vulnerable by sexual indiscretions that compromise his inheritance.

Eliot finished "Brother Jacob" only a month before starting *Silas Marner*. In the story, the confectioner David steals and buries the guineas that were his mother's life savings. Detected by Jacob, David manages to rid himself of the pitchfork-wielding man-child by convincing him that the gold coins have turned into yellow lozenges of candy. David runs away to Jamaica, fails to win the supremacy over the black population he had imagined, returns to England and settles in the village of Grimsworth under the name Edward Freely. His attempts to pass himself off as the heir to a West Indian fortune and to marry a local girl are foiled by the appearance of Jacob, seeking sweets – a return of the past that comically enacts more serious themes Eliot would address in *Silas Marner*.

"Brother Jacob" represents the consumption of confections in England made from sugar produced with black labor in West Indian colonies.[15] The atmosphere of corruption in which Faux/Freely thrives is emphasized by the marketing of this unwholesome food and the insatiable desire for it on the part of the villagers. The consumption of sweets is implicitly compared to the consumption of romantic literature. David gets his ideas about the West Indies from the story of Inkle and Yarico, first popularized by Richard Steele in his paper, the *Spectator* (1711–14). David identifies with Inkle, a white man who seduces a West Indian princess and then betrays and sells her to increase his fortune. David dupes the "Grimsworth Desdemonas" with his false and fantastic stories about Jamaica because they conflate this exotic locale with other places described in romantic poetry like Byron's "The Corsair" (1814) and Thomas Moore's "Lalla Rookh" (1817). In this way, Eliot makes an implicit argument for the value of her own realist fiction. Consuming literature with no moral content is like consuming sweets with no nutritional value. The story, while comic, is as dark and despairing about the potential for human sympathy as "The Lifted Veil." No one comes out well, as David is exposed, the villagers turn on him and even Jacob cannot be said to have the narrator's sympathy.

Silas Marner

Like Faux/Freely, Silas Marner is a man who flees his past geographically and psychologically, fashioning for himself a new identity. While later characters such as Tito in *Romola* and Bulstrode in *Middlemarch* will do the same, "Brother Jacob" and *Silas Marner* suggest that in 1860, Eliot was particularly preoccupied with the subject of effacing origins and wanted to explore it from different perspectives. She was questioning the inevitability of the return of the repressed, or, as she prefers to call it, of the Nemesis.[16] The narrator of "Brother Jacob" sums up the story as "an admirable instance of the unexpected forms in which the great Nemesis hides herself" (BJ, Ch. 3). Eliot thought in similar terms about the story of Silas, writing to Blackwood: "The Nemesis is a very mild one" (*GEL*, III:382). In both cases, fate brings a kind of justice in the exposure of past wrongs in works that are notably free of any institutional forms of law or justice.

As told in a flashback, Silas leaves his home in a northern city where he had lived in a tight-knit evangelical community – known only as "the church in Lantern Yard" – because he is betrayed by his best friend and neither God nor the church provided the justice he deserved. Several plot developments turn on Silas's cataleptic "fits." The interpretation of his mysterious physical condition is emblematic of a society in transition from religious to scientific authority: "To have sought a medical explanation for this phenomenon would have been held by Silas himself, as well as by his minister and fellow-members, a willful self-exclusion from the spiritual significance that might lie therein" (*SM*, 1). The narrator tells us that Silas is a simple man, but his appearance and his fits make him mysterious to those around him and hence he is interpreted in a variety of conflicting ways.

In Lantern Yard, Silas's friend William Dane – as dishonest and despicable a character as David Faux – takes advantage of Silas's disability to frame him for a theft and then frightens the community by implying that Silas is possessed by the devil. The narrator reports: "Any resort to legal measures for ascertaining the culprit was contrary to the principles of the church in Lantern Yard, according to which prosecution was forbidden to Christians" (*SM*, 1). So the community takes matters into its own hands by drawing lots: "*The lots declared that Silas Marner was guilty*" (*SM*, 1). Subsequently, Silas's fiancée breaks off her engagement with him and instead marries William Dane. The once-hopeful young man leaves his trust in God and man behind and removes southward to an isolated spot in the "rich central plane" (*SM*, 1) of England outside the remote village of Raveloe. The absence of legal measures available to Silas marks a contrast to Eliot's representation of the institutions of justice in *Adam Bede* (in which Hetty is tried and sentenced) and in *The Mill* (in which complex law suits are at the heart of the plot). The effect is to enhance the isolation of the wrongly accused man and make him seem all the more like the remnant of "a disinherited race" (*SM*, 1).

This conflict between medical authority and religious and folk beliefs recurs when Silas, who has a knowledge of homeopathic remedies imparted to him by his mother, is first revered and then reviled for practicing his art in Raveloe. Having helped a local woman suffering from heart disease with a potion of foxglove, he is compared to "the Wise Woman at Tarley," a figure resented by the local doctor, who told those who went to her that "they should have none of his help any more" (*SM*, 2). Having been typed as Satanic in his past life, Silas's knowledge now likens him to a witch, while his strange appearance and unexplained fits make him like a "dead man come to life again" and one whose soul went in and out of his body "like a bird out of its nest and back" (*SM*, Ch. 1).

The story begins fifteen years after Silas's exile from Lantern Yard. He lives only for his work as a weaver, hiding the money he amasses from his labor in the floor of his cottage. Living as a frugal miser, he takes his accumulated gold and silver coins out at night for a "revelry" in which he "spread them out in heaps and bathed his hands in them" (*SM*, 2). His spiritual, affectionate and even erotic love are all displaced on to the coins. He knows their faces intimately and would not think of parting with them. He is crushed when, in a reversal of the theft of which he was once accused, his carefully hidden treasure is stolen.

Whereas the theft in Lantern Yard served to exclude him from that community, his search for justice after the theft of his money is the beginning of his entry into the Raveloe community. At first these villagers promise to be no more likeable than those of "Brother Jacob," who believe that "when people came from nobody knew where, there was no knowing what they might do" (BJ, 2). A similar, if gentler, sarcasm is evident in *Silas Marner*: "How was a man to be explained unless you at least knew somebody who knew his father and mother?" (*SM*, 1). Like the inhabitants of Shepperton in "Amos Barton," however, the simple villagers of Raveloe prove capable of sympathy for a fellow human being in distress, no matter how much they had reviled him in the past.

The other story comprising the closely interwoven plots of *Silas Marner* is that of the local squire and his spoiled sons. Dunsey is particularly dissolute and inclined to blackmail his older brother Godfrey with his knowledge of the latter's secret marriage to a lower-class woman. Godfrey and Dunsey Cass's conflicted relationship seems to be resolved when Dunsey disappears, taking Godfrey's secret with him. For most of the story, the profligate Dunsey is assumed to have run away and no one connects his disappearance with the theft of Silas's gold.

As in Lantern Yard, there is no justice for Silas in Raveloe, and he is forced to endure desolate loneliness, having lost his only companions with his coins. But through his pitiable misfortune, the villagers become aware of him as someone other than a stranger with the witch-like knowledge and power to cast mysterious spells on them. When, following another cataleptic fit, a golden haired girl appears mysteriously in his cottage on a New Year's eve, the weaver takes it as a sign from God. He re-enters the community to plead for help but refuses to give her up and insists on raising her himself.

The most touching scenes in the novel come in the portrayal of Silas's growing love for the child. The former miser gradually softens into a feeling for human bonds that he had rejected after his early experience of betrayal as he learns to care for, educate, and even (hopelessly) discipline her. Eppie, whom he names after his sister, brings him into contact with the local people he had previously shunned, especially the practical matron Dolly Winthrop and her little boy Aaron. His integration into the community confirms Eliot's belief in the transforming, sustaining power of human fellowship and love, in direct contrast to the exacting religion to which Silas had once adhered. Rather than feel oppressed by her narrow society, like Maggie Tulliver, Eppie is content with her class and her life, marrying Aaron, her lifelong playmate.

Godfrey has known all along that Eppie is his child and that the woman found dead in the snow outside the weaver's door on the night Eppie appeared was his wife. But he cannot bring himself to tell his second wife, the conventionally proper Nancy Lammeter. It is sixteen years before a local stone pit full of water is drained and Dunsey's skeleton, along with Silas's gold, is unearthed. With the revelation of this crime, Godfrey feels that it is time to expose another, equally long-concealed secret – his paternity. Since he and Nancy have remained childless, and she has refused the possibility of adoption, Godfrey longs to reclaim Eppie, and Nancy must accept the reality of her husband's past sins, which she does with a stoic dignity that bestows a depth previously lacking in her character.

The themes of *Silas Marner*, "Brother Jacob", and "The Lifted Veil" suggest numerous parallels with Eliot's life between 1859 and 1860. She had forever left behind her life as Mary Ann Evans in the Midlands and refashioned herself as Marian Lewes in London. After 1856 she would never return to the homes of her youth and early adulthood, and she created continuity between her past and present lives through her imagination and her fiction. On 15 March 1859, her sister Chrissey died. Unwillingly estranged from each other by their brother Isaac, the sisters had no opportunity for reconciliation. On 21 March Eliot wrote to Sara Hennell: "Chrissey's death has taken from me the possibility of many things towards which I looked with some hope and yearning in the future" (*GEL*, III:38). At the end of that month, she presented Blackwood with "The Lifted Veil" about a man robbed of the possibility for hope by unwanted powers of foresight.

She took her epigraph for *Silas Marner* from Wordsworth's poem, "Michael": "A child, more than all other gifts / That earth can offer to declining man, / Brings hope with it, and forward-looking thoughts." The quotation offers hope for the future, though the story told in "Michael" is a sad one of disappointment and loss. Her ambiguous thoughts about the impossibility of closure in life and fiction are evident at the end of *Silas Marner* when Silas and Eppie return to Lantern Yard only to find it obliterated by a factory. No one remembers the community that had formed Silas's early self and no justice is possible. But in contrast to "Brother Jacob," which shows that remaking oneself can be a form of dishonesty, *Silas Marner* suggests that it can also be psychologically necessary for survival.

In *Romola,* the Italian novel to which she returned after the unplanned detour of *Silas Marner,* Romola's brother Dino rejects his past and his relations to follow his calling as a monk, an act his father views as betrayal. Romola's husband Tito, remaking himself from a Greek orphan into a political operative in Savonarola's Florence, is hounded by the adopted father whose betrayal was necessary to his success. Having released the optimistic side of her belief in the potential for human fellowship in *Silas Marner,* she delved deeply into the psychology of deceit in *Romola.*

Romola

Although all of George Eliot's novels are set in a period prior to their composition, *Romola* is her "historical novel." It attempts to recreate the sights, sounds, culture and politics of Florence at the end of the fifteenth century when the visionary Dominican monk Girolamo Savonarola (1452–1498) gained spiritual influence over many Florentines. Like Sir Walter Scott, Eliot painted her fictional characters into an historical tableau. She showed the ways in which individual lives are influenced, if not determined, by external events, writing of her two main characters: "as in the tree that bears a myriad of blossoms, each single bud with its fruit is dependent on the primary circulation of the sap, so the fortunes of Tito and Romola were dependent on certain grand political and social conditions which made an epoch in the history of Italy" (*R*, II:21). Her challenge was to make these characters and grand conditions historically accurate and also compelling to her Victorian readers.

Eliot's first four books had been extremely popular, so it was no wonder that the publisher George Smith of Smith, Elder & Co. set out to woo her from Blackwood. Smith offered £10,000 to serialize her as-yet-unwritten historical novel in his journal, the *Cornhill Magazine.* The amount was enormous and unprecedented, a landmark in publishing history as the largest sum ever offered for a novel until that time. After negotiations, Eliot took £7,000 for the copyright of *Romola,* which was to be published in twelve monthly parts.[17] The move to

Smith, Elder & Co. (which would bring out the novel after its serialization) was significant because it was the first and only book that Eliot did not publish with Blackwood. It was also awkward, as Blackwood had expected that he would publish the Italian novel, and he was not given the chance to make a counter-offer. He predicted rightly that his defected star author's new partnership would not be satisfactory for either side. Although many of her contemporaries, such as Dickens and Trollope, preferred to serialize their novels in magazines, Eliot disliked meeting the monthly deadlines. In the end, *Romola* did not achieve the success on which Smith had counted to revive sales of the *Cornhill* and was Eliot's only major financial failure.

Eliot's ambition to represent an "epoch in the history of Italy" that was marked by political upheaval, spiritual intensity and artistic productivity was inspired by a trip to Florence in 1860 and necessitated a return in 1861. To tell the story of Romola de' Bardi, the daughter of the classical scholar Bardo de' Bardi, and Tito Melema, adopted son of the classical scholar Baldassarre, Eliot turned scholar herself. She spent months reading histories of the period as well as contemporary writings such as the sermons of Savonarola, the poetry of Angelo Poliziano (1454–1494) and the political writing of Niccolo Machiavelli (1469–1527), all of whom figure in the novel. She also read deeply in the classical literature that was revived and revered during the Italian Renaissance and which offered an alternative, humanist world view to the religious fervor of Savonarola. She filled notebooks with her findings, and refers to at least a hundred actual historical persons in the novel.[18] Her consuming research led Lewes to caution that a Romance was not "the product of an Encyclopaedia" (*GEL*, III:474).[19]

While writing, she referred to *Romola* as a "romance," but despite what she admitted were "romantic and symbolic elements" (*GEL*, IV:104), the work is best understood as a realist novel. The setting depended on a careful reconstruction from the sources she studied at the Magliabecchian Library in Florence and in the British Library. Her appreciation for written texts as the primary means by which the past is preserved and transmitted becomes thematic in the novel. Bardo has devoted his life to studying the past and yet, as he complains:

> . . . that great work in which I had desired to gather, as into a firm web, all the threads that my research had laboriously disentangled, and which would have been the vintage of my life, was cut off by the failure of my sight and my want of a fitting coadjutor. (*R*, I:5)

Referring to his son Dino's decision to become a monk rather than a scholar, Bardo's excuses are those of a bitter man; yet his disappointment is one Eliot understood and feared. As an author aspiring to recreate the past in her own "great work," she was aware of the difficulties and pitfalls associated with weaving a web (one of her favorite metaphors) out of the threads of knowledge. Like her misguided scholar Mr Casaubon in *Middlemarch*, Bardo is known for his failure to produce a great work and is spoken of as "one of those scholars who lie overthrown in their learning, like cavaliers in heavy armour, and then get angry because they are over-ridden – " (*R*, I:13). Such joking about unrealized ambition reflects what was a very serious matter: Eliot's extreme doubt about whether she would be able to realize her own ambitions. Failures to see, hear and grasp a past world are written into the novel: in Bardo's blindness (literal and figurative) and in Baldassarre's fading memory with its tantalizing glimpses of a language he once understood but which now eludes him.

Eliot doubted whether her studies would enable her to bring Renaissance Florence alive, and she struggled to see the world she wanted to recreate. In her journal she wrote of the "oppressive sense of the far-stretching task" before her, of her "impending discouragement," and "distrust" in herself: "Will it ever be finished – ever be worth anything?"[20] Blackwood observed that Eliot's trouble was that she "hears her characters talking" and thinks they should be speaking Italian (*GEL*, III:427). In trying to bring the past to life, hearing is as important as seeing, and in addition to Bardo's blindness, she shows Baldassarre "visited by whispers which died out mockingly as he strained his ear after them" (*R*, II:30). Trying to recall at once his former self and a past world, Baldassarre epitomizes the failure to do both. When he is challenged to prove his identity as a scholar and Tito's father, he can only stare at the "fine Florentine Homer": "His eyes wandered over the pages that lay before him, and then fixed on them with a straining gaze" (*R*, II:39). This straining of ears and eyes was close to what Eliot experienced figuratively and literally while writing the novel.

Her anxiety was high in proportion to her expectations. *Romola* marked a departure from her previous writing in multiple ways. It was her first novel that was not set in nineteenth-century England and it was the first work in which achievement of an artistic goal became more important than communicating with readers. She explained to Sara Hennell: "I am under no external pressure to write anything which there is no strong internal reason for me to write" (*GEL*, IV:28). She also confessed to Hennell that "the book is addressed to fewer readers than my previous works" and was never intended to be "as 'popular' in the same sense as the others" (*GEL*, IV:49). Her research took her far beyond what would have been required to impress most readers with an authentic sense of place. It also went beyond that of her predecessors in the historical novel genre, Scott, G. P. R. James and Edward Bulwer Lytton. What mattered to Eliot was that *she* knew that her geographical and architectural descriptions, her political and sartorial details, her literary and theological allusions were historically correct. She admitted to Frederic Leighton, the acclaimed artist who provided illustrations for *Romola*: "Approximate truth is the only truth attainable, but at least one must strive for that, and not wade off into arbitrary falsehood" (*GEL*, IV:43). She had come as close to representing the past as it was possible for a novelist to do, and she judged the novel by her own standards, ultimately wondering how anyone could think she had written anything better than *Romola*.

In contrast to the exhausting task of historical recreation, the novel's psychological realism was the product of the author's experience and observations, following from the premise expressed in the Proem that "we still resemble the men of the past more than we differ from them" (*R*, Proem). The situations and characters are more complex than in previous novels. Her psychological portraits are more probing and disturbing. Themes familiar from *The Mill on the Floss*, such as the struggle between personal desire and social obligations, recur. The temptations to deception and the inevitability of exposure, not to mention the inclination of a privileged young man to take a mistress of a lower class, recall *Adam Bede* and *Silas Marner*. We can also see new elements that Eliot would develop in later novels, for example, the torments of a miserable marriage, which she would explore in *Middlemarch* and *Daniel Deronda*. *Romola*, then, is continuous with Eliot's other writings; and yet it is unique. As the result of Eliot's research and maturing skills as a novelist, *Romola* was unprecedented, and remains unsurpassed in its combination of factual reconstruction and imaginative invention, its breadth of historical understanding and keenness of psychological insight.

The remoteness of the setting and the perceived over-learnedness of the novel may be reasons for its relative unpopularity. Trollope, who admired *Romola*, consoled Eliot for its poor sales with the assurance that it would live after her: "The very gifts which are most sure to secure present success are for the most part antagonistic to permanent vitality" (*GEL*, VIII:311). In this case he was wrong. Unlike other erudite failures of the nineteenth century, such as *Moby Dick* (1851), *Romola* has not been fully appreciated in modern times and is still Eliot's least read novel. Yet *Romola* need not be intimidating, and repays the effort required to enter the world of Eliot's "man of the fifteenth century" (*R*, Proem).

Eliot could expect her readers to have some familiarity with Italian history. Renaissance Italy in particular fascinated many Victorians, who looked back at Renaissance Florence just as fifteenth century Florentines looked back on Ancient Athens. The writings and paintings of Dante Gabriel Rossetti and the

"Pre-Raphaelite Brotherhood" were well known, as were novels with Renaissance Italian settings, such as Harriet Beecher Stowe's *Agnes of Sorrento* (also serialized in the *Cornhill* in1862). The resurgence of Italian nationalism in the 1850s with charismatic leaders such as Garibaldi, Cavour and Mazzini also appealed to many of Eliot's contemporaries. Elizabeth Barrett Browning, for example, wrote "Casa Guidi Windows" (1851), which Eliot read before writing *Romola*. Eliot saw Mazzini in London and her stepson Thornie wrote home from boarding school in 1860 imagining that he might run away to become the liberator of Sicily to make the world ring with the glory of the names "Garibaldi, Türr and Thornton Lewes" (*GEL*, VIII:271). The romance of Italy was pervasive in Victorian popular culture.[21]

Eliot weaves into the novel much of the historical information needed to understand its plot. She defines words and provides footnotes. She uses the densely written Proem to set the historical scene in which a fifteenth century "shade," imagined to have died just before the start of the novel's action, asks the questions that the novel will then answer: "How has it all turned out?" (*R*, Proem). What has become of Lorenzo de' Medici's son and successor Piero? With which foreign power has Florence allied? France? Or Naples? What has become of Savonarola, the monk who wanted to reform the Church and Papacy by making an example of Florence, ending the corrupt Medici domination and establishing a democratic but Christian state? *Romola* details events that occurred after Piero fled, the French invaded, and Savonarola came to power, a period spanning from Lorenzo's death in 1492 to Savonarola's death in 1498. The fictional Tito, a charming, enigmatic Greek outsider with no loyalties to any of the contending Florentine parties, tries to advance himself politically by playing the dangerous game of a triple agent, appearing alternately to support the pro-Medici party, Savonarola, and the Compagnacci who opposed both. His corruption occurs during a corrupt period, but the personal betrayals that mirror his political betrayals reveal that it is his character even more than historical circumstances that leads him down this self-destructive path.

Within this political context is the context of intellectual factions or opposing world views that existed at this time. Late fifteenth century Florence was characterized simultaneously by a secular, humanistic sensibility informed by classical literature and art, and a Christian world view, which in Bardo's opinion knows of "no past older than the missal and the crucifix" (*R*, I:5). Bardo is bitter against the Christianity that seduced his son Dino away from him, while Dino (now known as Fra Luca) tells Romola that his father was "like one busy picking shining stones in a mine, while there was a world dying of plague above him" (*R*, I:15). These views are irreconcilable, dividing families as well as the state, but Eliot holds them in tension, presenting complexities. Essentially a rationalist, she sees that the scholar's fanaticism can be as futile as the religious fanatic's. Bardo, Baldassarre and Tito's classical learning provide no moral structure. Bardo lives in the past among "the parchment backs, the unchanging mutilated marble, the bits of obsolete bronze and clay" (*R*, I:5), and has little sympathy with his youthful, loving daughter.

While representing Savonarola as a fanatic, Eliot does not dismiss some of his basic Christian beliefs, and sees good in the "terror of the unseen" and "the initial recognition of a moral law restraining desires" (*GEL*, I:11). Christianity provides moral guidance, but in its extreme form cuts its followers off from ancient traditions, as illustrated by Savonarola's Bonfire of the Vanities in which invaluable books recording that past are burned. The moral flaw in an unbending adherence to laws is evident when Savonarola sends Romola back to Tito. Romola wonders where her duty to the institution of marriage ends and her duty to herself and what she perceives as right begins.

Interestingly, what unifies these different groups is their sense of identity as Florentines and their desire to do what is best for Florence, even though they differ on what that might be. Savonarola thinks the city and republic need a moral scourging, but he knows enough, in sending Romola back to Florence, to appeal to her identity as a Florentine: "And doubtless you were taught how there were pagan women who felt what it was to live for the Republic; yet you have never felt that you, a Florentine woman, should live for Florence" (*R*, II:40). This sense of corporate identity is part of what attracted Eliot to the subject of her novel. The shade who looks down on the city in the Proem lived an active and passionate political life "which could belong only to a narrow scene of corporate action," where men "set their eyes every day on the memorials of their commonwealth" (*R*, Proem). The period of the Florentine Republic intrigued Eliot because it had national, indeed international, political drama within "walls of six miles' circuit" (*R*, Proem). Florentines like Nello the barber looked upon their little patch as "the navel of the earth" because they knew that great and important ideas were being fought for before their eyes.

Eliot's English fiction had already shown that she was interested in microcosms, in the isolated towns and villages in which the most elemental human passions might be found: love, jealousy, ambition, murderous hatred, healing compassion. And yet, the petty scandals of "Amos Barton," the dissenting politics of "Janet's Repentance," the lawsuits of Mr Tulliver, or the robbing of Silas Marner have no importance beyond the "narrow, ugly, groveling existence" of these provincial people (*Mill*, IV:1). While Hetty is tried at the regional assizes, the consequences of her crime and her conviction affect no one beyond her small circle. The Florentines under the Medici, and then in the struggles to stabilize their fledgling commonwealth, offered sentiments and allegiances on a larger, nobler scale. Tom Tulliver's oath on the family bible in early nineteenth-century England can only be viewed as primitive and tribal. In contrast, the loyalty to Florence felt and enacted by Bernardo del Nero, Savonarola and Romola was of the ennobling, national kind that looked beyond self.

Eliot would not venture beyond what she knew to be the limitations of her scope – to battlefields or court politics on the scale of her much-admired Walter Scott. Ingeniously, she found the historical time and place that would allow her to exercise her talents at portraying the local while still managing to address the "grand" social conditions and themes that increasingly characterize her writing. In *Middlemarch*, she located sublime tragedy in the absence of a "coherent faith and order which could perform the function of knowledge for the ardently willing soul" (*MM*, Prelude), but in *The Spanish Gypsy* and *Daniel Deronda*, characters seem to be searching for something that might provide the corporate identity that the fifteenth century Florentines, whether religious or secular, took for granted as what was most noble in their natures. Loyalty to a higher cause or even to others is what Tito lacks: he betrays his father; he betrays his wife both sexually and by selling her father's library. He holds nothing sacred. He is Eliot's idea of a moral monster, an illustration of why the bonds of duty, affection, and patriotism are supremely human.

Eliot's increasing concern with the preservation and inheritance of culture reflected her role as a writer aspiring to use collective and personal memory to fashion art that spoke to the present. *Romola* is a turning point. There is little evidence in *Adam Bede* of the importance of cultural transmission through inherited texts, though Adam is literate and does work to educate himself. In *The Mill on the Floss*, all attempts to turn Tom into a "scholard" fail miserably, but we see an inkling of the power of inherited texts in Maggie's copy of Thomas à Kempis. In *Silas Marner*, human bonds form the community with no thought to literary, textual traditions.

Beginning with *Romola*, Eliot is not only transmitting culture by using the past to make art for the future, she is making that process itself central to the themes and plots of her novels, which become preoccupied with inheritance laws, wills, aborted scholarship, as well as successful transmissions, such as that of Jewish culture from Mordecai to Daniel Deronda. *Romola* signaled a mid-career transition in which Eliot would experiment with verse and drama, eventually finding her way back to the English stories with which she began her career. But her sense of purpose and of audience, even her writing style, would be altered by the process – both exasperating and exhilarating – of making the past speak to the present.

Felix Holt, The Radical

George Eliot viewed *Romola* as a "well-defined transition in her life." She claimed: "I began it a young woman, – I finished it an old woman."[22] The changes that occurred in the novelist's perspective as a result of writing *Romola* may be seen in her next novel, *Felix Holt, The Radical* (1866). Often called Eliot's "political novel," it is a transitional work that prepares for the broad social canvas of *Middlemarch* by addressing the most profound personal and political questions she had yet attempted in an English story. The moral outlook is sterner, the critique of social institutions more radical, and while for most readers the characters in *Felix Holt* are less appealing than those in *Middlemarch*, the novel presents a starker version of George Eliot's moral and political positions at mid-career precisely because she had not yet achieved the complexity and sophistication of her mature style.

First mentioned in Eliot's diary of 28 March 1865, *Felix Holt* is set in the Midlands during the months immediately following the passing of the first Reform Bill (September 1832 – April 1833). The geography and time frame return to those of *Scenes, Adam Bede, The Mill on the Floss* and *Silas Marner*, making the changes that occurred in the author while she dwelt imaginatively in Renaissance Italy – writing with what she called her "best blood" – apparent by contrast (*GEL*, VI:335–6). The book insists on the importance of making the difficult rather than the easy choices in life. Its heroine, Esther Lyon, faces a choice between "moral mediocrity," complacency, and wealth on the one hand and moral improvement, self-knowledge, and poverty on the other. That this decision takes the form of selecting a husband reflects limitations on women at the time; it also represents Eliot's increasing interest in showing how "incalculable is the effect of one personality on another" (*FH*, II:22).

The theme of choice resonates at both the public and the private level. Esther must choose between the man whom she believes will challenge her to be a better person (Felix Holt) and the man who can fulfill her girlish dream of becoming a fine lady but who offers no moral challenge (Harold Transome). On a larger scale, *Felix Holt* represents Britain too as facing a choice: address the deep social ills of ignorance and poverty or gloss over them by extending the franchise based on an arbitrary standard of land holding. With the first Reform Bill, the nation chose the latter, easier option. Felix Holt is radical in his belief that the franchise and political reform generally are distractions from the pressing need to educate the working population and to arrest the degradation and stagnation that follow from its ignorance and propensity to find solace from poverty in drink. Education and moral reform are the only means by which men can elevate themselves above poverty and escape the mindset that submits to oppression. Felix's views, which may be seen as reflective of Eliot's own, are radical in their critique of democracy; they question the value of representation for the uneducated majority. The politics of the novel, however, involve more than Felix's views and must be evaluated in the context of its complexly interrelated plots.

In 1868, Blackwood, a Scottish Tory, prevailed upon Eliot to write an essay in the voice of Felix Holt that would elaborate on what he assumed to be Felix's sound conservative principles, and thereby contribute to the current debates about the second Reform Bill (1867). Somewhat reluctantly, Eliot wrote "Address to the Working Men, by Felix Holt" (*Blackwood's Magazine*, January 1868). Understandably, the essay is often used to interpret *Felix Holt*. But the freestanding essay appears more conservative than the novel when we consider the romance and inheritance plots that reveal the latter's radical skepticism about the stability and viability of traditional British class structures.

As in most of Eliot's fiction, the narrator provides the perspective of the present, evaluating the action with the benefit of hindsight, and so we are told that Felix's reservations about the first Reform Bill were justified: "At that time, when faith in the efficacy of political change was at fever-heat in ardent Reformers, many measures which men are still discussing with little confidence on either side, were then talked about and disposed of like property in near reversion" (*FH*, II:16). The notion of reversion foreshadows the plot in which Transome Court "reverts" to the "lineal issue" of the Bycliffes, but the main thrust of the comment is that reformers oversimplified complex problems and pronounced them solved by the Reform Bill. In fact, according to the narrator, the consequences of Reform over the past thirty years have not been "wisdom and happiness," but rather "doubt and despondency" (*FH*, II:16).

The narrator's views are also apparent in the ironic use of the language of equality that drives Reform. Several scenes are set in public houses and drunkenness is a major concern in the novel. The "publics" are patronized along political lines, as the narrator observes: "the company at the Blue Cow was of an inferior kind – equal, of course, in the fundamental attributes of humanity, such as desire for beer, but not equal in ability to pay for it" (*FH*, I:11). Voting and drinking (in the form of candidate "treating") are inseparable, and while Felix preaches against such corruption, the narrator remains sarcastic: "In the great Reform-year, Hope was mighty: the prospect of Reform had even served the voters instead of drink; . . .'" (*FH*, II:16). Belief in Reform – an unfounded hope – is compared to the intoxicating effects of alcohol, and the implication is that this class of new voter must be appeased with one or another form of intoxicant.

Felix is determined to remain in the artisan class. He is disdainful of social climbing and skeptical about the value of the vote for the working classes. But Felix, merely a "voteless man of ideas" (*FH*, II:16), holds little interest for politicians such as Harold Transome, who is running for a seat in Parliament as a Radical. The irony of value being bestowed on a man because he has the vote, rather than the vote being bestowed because the man has value, is illustrated in the case of the voteless Felix and also in the comic descriptions of the voters. Timothy Rose, the newly enfranchised gentleman farmer from Leek Malton, ventures out on election morning "to go through this ordeal as early as possible" (*FH*, II:31). Leaving home with some "foreboding," having "wavered in his intention to vote," he does the deed and thus comes "up to the level of his times" (*FH*, II:31). He then confesses, or boasts, that he has cast two votes that cancel each other out and upon being told that he "might as well have stayed at home and not voted at all," he protests that "the most a independent man can do is to try and please all" (*FH*, II:31). It is with such humor and distance from the common man that the narrator illustrates some of the absurd consequences of enfranchising those so ill prepared for the privilege.

The ironic tone runs throughout the more serious descriptions of drunkenness and mob violence that end in one man's death and in Felix's arrest. In describing the disreputable electioneering agent, Mr Johnson, with the "many-mixed motives" that lead him to take some pleasure in his employer, Mr Jermyn's, downfall, the narrator observes: "No system, religious or political, I believe, has laid it down as a principle that all men are alike virtuous, or even that all the people rated for £80 houses are an honour to their species" (*FH*, III:37). The question of value and honor is again underscored by references to this arbitrary way of "rating" citizens.

Just as the novel may be seen as politically conservative because it appears to oppose the extension of the franchise, it may seem anti-feminist because Esther's personal reform comes by way of submission to Felix. Yet in Esther, Eliot sought to show an instance of moral choice in one who recognized the potential for moral influence, as did the author herself. When Eliot faced the death of her father in 1849, for example, she feared losing part of her "moral nature" and turning "earthly sensual and devilish for want of that purifying restraining influence" (*GEL*, I:284). It is significant that she dedicated the manuscript of *Felix Holt* to George Henry Lewes in "this thirteenth year of their united life, in which the deepening sense of her own imperfectness has the consolation of their deepening love."[23] The dedication reflects ideas addressed in the novel: Eliot believed that Lewes made her a better person, but she never stopped struggling with what she felt to be her own imperfection. Esther, in her more superficial but nonetheless genuine way – and like later heroines such as Dorothea and

Gwendolen – also wants to be better. She may appear to "lean on" Felix, but her soul-searching is independent of him, reflective of her private desire to be the better person she instinctively feels she can become. If Felix were to love her, "her life would be exalted into something quite new – into a sort of difficult blessedness, such as one may imagine in beings who are conscious of painfully growing into possession of higher powers" (*FH*, II:22). Esther's ambition to be a "fine lady" has transformed into an ambition to improve, in the words of her father, "the soul of a man and the character of a citizen" (*FH*, II:16).

Esther is also influenced by her observations of Mrs Transome, whose ruined life seems to be a living out of the fine ladyism that Esther initially desires. Like Esther, the young Miss Lingon refused to take moral questions seriously, and paid the price for her frivolity. The narrator observes of Miss Lingon that "the notion that what is true and, in general, good for mankind, is stupid and drug-like, is not a safe theoretic basis in circumstances of temptation and difficulty" (*FH*, I:1). Miss Lingon married for the wrong reasons, choosing a husband (Mr Transome) who brought her social status but was unable to help her realize her better self. She then took refuge from her marriage with a man (Jermyn) whose moral vulgarity would only entangle her in a web of lies and deceptions. Raising Jermyn's illegitimate son Harold as the legitimate son of Mr Transome is a lie that made her later conniving with Jermyn to conceal the rightful heirs of Transome Court seem trivial. When Esther visits Transome Court with the knowledge that she is entitled legally to inherit it, the "dimly suggested tragedy" of Mrs Transome's life afflicts her "even to horror": "It seemed to have come as a last vision to urge her towards the life where the draughts of joy sprang from the unchanging fountains of reverence and devout love" (*FH*, III:50). She searches for those fountains by rejecting Harold and accepting Felix. Unlike Felix, who initially vows that he will never marry, Esther seems unable to conceive of moral improvement without him. As the narrator observes, "In the ages since Adam's marriage, it has been good for some men to be alone, and for some women also. But Esther was not one of these women" (*FH*, III:44).

The political themes of *Felix Holt* circulate through the novel, resulting in a broad social critique more subtly, even playfully, developed than in Eliot's earlier work. Her own radicalism may be found in her questioning of the class hierarchy, her exposure of institutions based on blood, land, and inheritance as fundamentally unstable, arbitrary, and false. While she sees it as folly that certain unqualified men should be allowed to exercise new influence through the vote, she also exposes the absurdity – the randomness and chance – of the class hierarchy generally. That power relations are not always what they seem is evident in the master/servant relationships. The narrator describes Jermyn in relation to Mrs Transome as the man "who was to pass with those nearest to her as her indebted servant, but whose brand she secretly bore" (*FH*, I:9). Dominick is invaluable to Harold, as Christian is to Philip Debarry. Denner knows her place, but is nonetheless far more than servant to Mrs Transome, who calls her "the creature in the world that loves me best" (*FH*, III:39). The emphasis on servants, their invisible power and intimacy with those they serve, is relatively rare in Eliot's fiction, though devoted female servants appear in *The Mill on the Floss* (Keziah), *Middlemarch* (Tantripp) and *Daniel Deronda* (Miss Merry). The male factotum also plays a central role in *Deronda* (Lush) and is mocked in *Impressions* (Pummel). She addressed the question of servants directly, if ironically, in her essay "Servant's Logic" (1865).

But these figures and the inverted hierarchies they represent are more important in *Felix Holt* than in any other novel and are part of its thematic unity. The machinations of literal servants such as Christian and metaphoric servants such as Jermyn combine with scenes like the "select Olympian feast in the apartment of the cook" to give the novel a carnivalesque quality. Their presence is part of the larger theme of disrupted order threatened by the extension of the franchise: if given the vote, the majority lower orders will rule the country. The pivotal narrative roles played by servants such as Christian and Scales are a formal expression of this chaotic scenario. As the working classes discuss politics in the pubs, we are aware that new voters could tip the scales of the election. They are playing an unwitting role in reversing the traditional order, just as it is initially an "unconscious Christian" who helps to expose Esther's position as the "unconscious remainder-man" waiting to reverse the fortunes of the Transomes.

Eliot's attitude toward these inversions and reversals of traditional structures is ambiguous. The novel suggests that chaos is at the foundation of the ordered British class system. The plot ultimately reveals that there may be only a legal technicality, an undisclosed secret or lost document, standing between a family's possession of an estate – and the political power that entails – and poverty that would disenfranchise its members. Harold's turning Radical after taking a Greek slave as his wife; the exposure of the fraudulent means by which the Transomes have held on to their land; and the bizarre coincidences by which the blackmailing Christian forces the issue into the light are all part of what has been criticized as Eliot's overly complicated plot. But the complicated legalities have a thematic significance. Any simple notion that aristocrats own the land and hand it down to their offspring disappears in the chaos of sold rights, "base fees," and "remainder-men," legal terms which nonetheless suggest the monetary (rather than the noble familial) basis of land ownership. The old system of granting votes only to land owners is as arbitrary and as crass as extending the vote to ten pound free holders.

The spectre of illegitimate children (Harold) and imbecility (Mr Transome, Durfey Transome, and Tommy Trounsen) further debases the identities of the landed class and undermines the notion that such classes rule by anything nobler than chance. The degrees of luck and strategy involved in the game of power are represented in metaphors of games, most famously chess. Chess represents the combination of luck and cunning whereby Jermyn was able to use the law to keep Transome Court in the hands of the Transomes, though the fantasy of Eliot's famous metaphor (Chapter 24) is precisely one of inversion, one in which the "men" have ideas of their own and "you might be beaten by your own pawns" (*FH*, II:29).

Whereas Jermyn's approach to the game of life is to manipulate men like Johnson to his own advantage, Mrs Transome's guilty wish that her first child should die to make room for Harold is the type of desire that makes life a

> . . . hideous lottery, where every day may turn up a blank; where men and women who have the softest beds and the most delicate eating, who have a very large share of that sky and earth which some are born to have no more of than the fraction to be got in a crowded entry, yet grow haggard, fevered, and restless, like those who watch in other lotteries.
>
> (*FH*, I:1)

Mrs Transome, born with a large share of the sky and earth, plays a lottery that is part of a larger lottery in which one is born wealthy or poor. In contrast to the intricately ordered battle of wits implied by chess, the lottery depends entirely on luck and appropriately symbolizes the conflict between the passion of Mrs Transome's desires and her impotence to satisfy them. The unhappy desire at the center of her life is likened to the gambler's fever to win, restlessly yet passively watching in "other lotteries."

The novel does not suggest that the extension of the franchise caused such chaos. The Reform Bill, through Felix's eyes, is an irrelevant ruse. The novel shows that the chaos feared by conservatives who oppose extending the franchise was always already there, always the state of British class and power relations; a mere turn of the wheel, a ticket in the lottery, or a cunning move in chess might reverse the most established social order. Such a reversal of fortune does occur in the novel when Esther stands to inherit. By exposing the arbitrary way in which privilege and status are conferred and maintained, the novel offers a model of radical equality, which makes Esther's choice of renunciation crucial. In the tradition of other heroines who reject money and status, such as Eppie in *Silas Marner* and Dorothea in *Middlemarch*, Esther takes the element of chance out of her life: takes the control that will allow her to shape her own destiny, opt out of the "hideous lottery" and discover, as Felix says, "that there's some dignity and happiness for a man other than changing his station" (*FH*, III:45).

Poetry

When George Eliot sent Blackwood a packet of poems on 6 March 1874 and instructed him on when and how to publish them, she explained that "every one of those I now send you represents an idea which I care for strongly and wish to propagate as far as I can" (*GEL*, VI:26). The poems were published as *The Legend of Jubal and Other Poems* (1874), and Blackwood remarked that he was impressed by their "warning voice," adding, "if you have any lighter pieces written before the sense of what a great author should do for mankind came so strongly upon you, I should like much to look at them" (*GEL*, VI:37). His tone is ironic, almost teasing, but there is little in Eliot's poetry that encourages levity or suggests self-irony.

Eliot's poetry, much of it written between the publications of *Felix Holt* (1866) and *Middlemarch* (1871–2), has presented a long-standing critical problem. The poems cannot compare to the novels as contributions to literature, but they were popular enough in Eliot's lifetime and were obviously important to her. Reading the poems today, anyone familiar with her novels may well ask why she persisted in writing them and whether her own and Lewes's critical faculties were clouded when evaluating their merit and insisting on their publication. Two factors are worth considering when trying to understand why Eliot wrote the poetry that she did, and this exchange with Blackwood sums them up well. One was that she had ideas that she wished to "propagate" and the other was that she had a "sense of what a great author should do for mankind." These two things are related to each other and also to the form of poetry.[24]

Eliot often spoke of her novels in terms of the influence she wanted them to have on readers. Her novels have been called novels of ideas, but rarely do we think of her complex and subtle "experiments in life" as being written to propagate specific ideas. The major themes in her poetry can also be found in her novels, but in the poems she intentionally distills ideas which in the novels are diffused in the larger artistic project of creating a realistic, multi-faceted fictional world. Additionally, to a Victorian author – even one whose novels were influential in transforming the genre into high art – the highest and most serious form of writing was poetry, and it seems as though, despite lacking the genius for composing verse that she had for writing prose, George Eliot felt that a great writer should write poetry. Perhaps it was a remnant of a previous generation's aesthetic and moral bias, recalling her youthful puritanical renunciation of novels as wicked. Or, perhaps Eliot simply could not feel herself the equal of contemporaries such as Tennyson, much less past greats such as Wordsworth, Scott, Goethe, Milton or Shakespeare, until she had tried her hand at both epic and lyric poetry.[25]

By freeing herself from the self-imposed restrictions of realism and conforming to the metrical requirements of poetry, Eliot expressed most purely a set of beliefs: in the need to strive for the high ideals of art in "The Legend of Jubal" (1870) and "Armgart" (1871); altruism in "Agatha" (1869) and "Armgart"; love in "How Lisa Loved the King" (1869); and corporate identity in *The Spanish Gypsy* (1868).[26] Rosemarie Bodenheimer compares "Armgart" (1871) to "the melodrama of opera" in which Eliot was able to "dramatize strong versions of single emotions as her prose narratives never do."[27] At the same time that her poems single out for emphasis ideas and emotions that are present in the novels, they also provide insight into what she thought poetry ought to be and do and in turn what she thought fiction should be and do. The poems help today's readers to remember that the aesthetic of realism as practiced by Eliot and the other major Victorian novelists co-existed with idealistic, mythical, even fantastical poetry, to which Eliot contributed.

George Eliot's first published poem was also her most ambitious and grandly conceived. Her epic poem *The Spanish Gypsy*, like *Romola*, was an historical recreation that required her to visit Spain, study Spanish, and research fifteenth century Spanish history. Gypsies appear in both *The Mill on the Floss* and the "Brother and Sister" sonnets (1874). It is clear from Maggie's fantasy about becoming Queen of the Gypsies that the nomadic people were a source of romance in the rural England of Eliot's youth. The function of Maggie's encounter with the Gypsies in *The Mill on the Floss*, however, is to dispel the fantasy with a dose of realism: the real Gypsies are unpoetic Gypsies in the same sense that the Cohens are unpoetic Jews in *Daniel Deronda*: they disappoint stereotypical expectations by being too human. It is significant that even in a novel as Wordsworthian as *The Mill on the Floss*, we see a persistent anti-Romantic strain. In *The Spanish Gypsy*, however, despite her research to get the details right, the verse form grants Eliot permission to indulge a romanticized portrait of the Gypsies as they sing, dance, and chant, "Like those broad-chested rovers of the night / Who pour exuberant strength upon the air."[28]

It may also be that she chose for her setting a remote time of dukes and minstrels and evil priests that not even historical research could render unpoetic. The dark shadow of the Inquisition is important as well to emphasize the atmosphere of intolerance and persecution that made the Gypsies' desire for a homeland especially urgent. *The Spanish Gypsy* foreshadows the concerns of *Daniel Deronda* and expresses them, as Eliot's poetry always does, in a more concentrated form: it is easier to understand persecution while the Inquisition is authorizing torture, murder, and warfare. Becoming Queen of the Gypsies in the fifteenth century may be easier to believe in than Daniel Deronda's vague nineteenth-century notion of "social captainship" (*DD*, VIII:63).

Like many of her other poems, *The Spanish Gypsy* centers on a woman's conflict between love and an even higher calling of corporate duty. The orphan Fedalma has been raised by Spaniards and, believing herself Spanish, is engaged to the Spaniard Don Silva. Yet she has an undefined yearning of heart and a seemingly inbred affiliation with the music and folk traditions of the Gypsies. Just before her marriage, she discovers that her father is the King of the dispersed Gypsies and that he wishes his daughter to fulfill his dream of leading the Gypsies out of Spain to a national homeland. Fedalma addresses her people:

> Your Chief is dying: I his daughter live
> To do his dying will. He asks you now
> To promise me obedience as your Queen,
> That we may seek the land he won for us,
> And live the better life for which he toiled.
>
> (IV)

Eliot conceived of the story originally as a play, thinking of the Greek tragedies or perhaps Shakespeare as a model. Fedalma's forsaking love to undertake this heroic task seemed suited to drama. And yet she never could finish the work as a play and agonized over it, writing in her journal: "Ill with bilious headache, and very miserable about my soul as well as my body. *George has taken my drama away from me.*"[29] One might call *The Spanish Gypsy*'s final form a verse novel but, in keeping with Eliot's sense of the appropriate subject and tone of great poetry, its themes and language are elevated – anything but the "language of men" with which her much-admired Wordsworth had sought to revolutionize poetry earlier in the nineteenth century. The one-volume edition of *The Spanish Gypsy* sold well, encouraging Eliot to write and publish other poems.

In "The Legend of Jubal" (written 1869–70), we see her turning to Genesis and imagining Jubal, a descendant of Cain, who discovered, or perhaps more accurately invented, music by listening to nature, to human voices and to the sound of his brother Tubal-cain's hammer:

> Jubal, too, watched the hammer, till his eyes,
> No longer following its fall or rise,
> Seemed glad with something that they could not see
> But only listed to – some melody,
> Wherein dumb longings inward speech had found,
> Won from the common store of struggling sound.
>
> (*Poetry* I, lines 247–53)

The biblical source marks an interesting stage in Eliot's relationship to both Christian and Jewish Scripture, which reached from her early Christian phase, to her translations of the German Higher Criticism of the Bible, to her study of Hebrew in preparation for *Daniel Deronda*. Throughout her work, biblical references are explicit in quotations and implicit in situations, but in "Jubal" she begins with a biblical context and invents her own myth, an allegory for the relationship of the artist to his art. There are many artists with complex functions in Eliot's novels – Philip Wakem, Piero de Cosimo, Adolf Naumann, Hans Meyrick, Julius Klesmer, the Princess Halm-Eberstein – but novels for Eliot were not a place for allegory, and "Jubal" is an example of how Eliot used poetry to clarify and propagate ideas that were important to her as well as relevant to her own role as an artist.

Like several other of her poems, recalling the work of Romantic poets like Keats and Shelley, "Jubal" is concerned with inspiration and the relationship of art to nature.[30] It considers the drive to create permanence – to counter the transience of life and to memorialize the dead – as a foundational element of art. The poem's mythic setting enhances its tragedy, which reflects the inconsequentiality of the artist relative to the independent life of the art:

> Come, let us fashion acts that are to be,
> When we shall lie in darkness silently,
> As young brother doth, whom yet we see
> Fallen and slain, but [reigning] in our will
> By that one image of him pale and still.
>
> (*Poetry* I, lines 126–30)

Consistent with ideas in one of her best-known poems, "Oh May I Join Choir Invisible" (1867), these lines suggest that the images of the dead remain with us and the desire to remember them is a motivation for art, as is the desire to make something by which we will be remembered.

The centrality of memory to art is also the theme of the "Brother and Sister" sonnets, a Shakespearean sonnet sequence reworking the same material that formed the basis of Book I of *The Mill on the Floss*. Like her fiction, Eliot's poetry is rarely personal or confessional. The early chapters of *The Mill on the Floss* and the "Brother and Sister" sonnets are the exceptions. Written over a period of months in 1869 while she was nursing Lewes's terminally ill son Thornton and beginning to write *Middlemarch*, the sonnets reveal just how important the childhood memories associated with the love of nature and of her brother were to her life and art. The rhymed couplet that ends the eleventh and final sonnet reads: "But were another childhood-world my share,/ I would be born a little sister there."

"Armgart" is another of the narrative poems that address the relationship of the artist to her art and which, like "Agatha" and "How Lisa Loved the King," scrutinize the conflicts experienced by women whose strength takes different forms. Its portrait of the female artist has attracted attention from feminist critics who have recognized it as Eliot's most powerful statement about the choices gifted women were asked to make. In the story of the great singer who loses her voice, Eliot focuses on the idea that in losing something we value, we may discover something more valuable still – a moral similar to that of *Silas Marner*. And yet the passion and anger of the main character's speeches suggest that such renunciation was far from an unambiguous good to Eliot:

> All the world now is but a rack of threads
> To twist and dwarf me into pettiness
> And basely feigned content, the placid mask
> Of women's misery.
> (*Poetry* I, lines 737–40)

Reminiscent of E. B. Browning's Aurora Leigh, Armgart turns down the offer of marriage to pursue her art. Unlike Aurora, however, she gets neither art nor marriage in the end. Despite Armgart's acceptance of a humble role as music teacher, her story is a bleak one of defeated ambition.

Armgart foreshadows no character in Eliot's fiction so much as the Princess Halm-Eberstein in *Daniel Deronda*. Both figures dramatize conflicts that Eliot felt as a female artist, conflicts between ambition and social notions of femininity (Armgart is "unwomaned") as well as between ambition and the desire to do the work for its own sake. Her short poem "Stradivarius" (1874) about the craftsman of violins addresses this directly. When challenged by an artist friend, Naldo, about his dull workman-like ways, Stadivarius replies:

> 'Twere purgatory here to make them ill;
> And for my fame – when any master holds
> 'Twixt chin and hand a violin of mine,
> He will be glad that Stradivari lived,
> Made violins, and made them of the best.
> (*Poetry* II, lines 87–90)

Here she upholds her ideal of the worker – especially the artisan like Adam Bede or Felix Holt – who takes pride in his work for its own sake.

The pattern of Eliot's writing career had always included diversions when she needed to rest her mind from the intensity of creating a new fictional world. "The Lifted Veil" was a break from writing *The Mill on the Floss*. *Silas Marner* thrust itself upon her as she was contemplating *Romola*. The period of experimentation with poetry was an expression of Eliot's desire to produce the poetic work that a great writer should. It was a way of propagating ideas about art without compromising the aesthetic principles of realism she applied to her fiction. It was also clearly a preparation for the emergence of her most mature and confident voice in her last two novels.

Eliot's poetry is full of musical artists but the only poet in her fiction is more enamored with the myth of the poet than with writing poetry. *Middlemarch*'s Will Ladislaw tells Dorothea that to be a poet is to have a soul "so quick to discern that no shade of quality escapes it. . . . a soul in which knowledge passes instantaneously into feeling, and feeling flashes back as a new organ of knowledge." To which Dorothea replies, "But you leave out the poems" (*MM*, II:22). Like Gwendolen in *Daniel Deronda*, who imagines she can become a singer without imagining the work it would require, Will lacks the discipline to become a poet. George Eliot, in contrast, worked diligently crafting verse to propagate ideas about art, ironically producing poetry that is characteristically fascinating for its ideas, but which has never been appreciated for its artistic achievement.

Middlemarch

George Eliot continued to write poetry even after she began a novel called *Middlemarch* in the summer of 1869. Progress on that novel was interrupted by the final illness and death of Thornie Lewes on 19 October 1869. For a year following the trauma of that experience, she wrote mainly poetry until a new story called "Miss Brooke" took over her imagination.[31] She wrote in her journal that she had completed 100 pages and added: "Poetry halts just now."[32] "Miss Brooke" did not displace the interrupted novel, but rather became part of it. By March of 1871, Eliot was making great progress on the multi-plot *Middlemarch* with the first of its eight books entitled "Miss Brooke."

The original core of the novel was the Vincy-Featherstone plot. It tells the story of young Fred Vincy, who has expectations of inheriting his uncle Featherstone's estate, and of his sister Rosamond who aspires to rise socially through marriage to the promising new-comer to Middlemarch, Tertius Lydgate. Both the Vincy-Featherstone plot and the plot recounting the courtship, marriage and widowhood of Dorothea Brooke are stories in which the naïve optimism of the young and eager encounters the manipulative power of the old and bitter. The interconnected plots are set in the town of Middlemarch in the English Midlands from the fall of 1829 to the spring of 1832. The first Reform Bill (1832) defines the political climate, as it had in *Felix Holt*, and reforms in medicine (Lydgate and the fever hospital), farming (represented by Caleb and Fred), housing (Dorothea's plans and Sir James's implementation of them) and transportation (the coming of the railway) contribute to the sense that men and women at every level of society believed in the "march" of progress. The narrator, speaking from and to the early 1870s – well into the reign of Queen Victoria that began in 1837 – has sufficient distance on this earlier generation to know what the new faith in science, technology and progress generally has been able to accomplish and also what it has not.

The novel's uniqueness comes from placing the town rather than an individual character at the center and from the authority of the omniscient narrator. The narrator, whose gender and age are unspecified, occupies a position between the past and future of the characters and speaks as though suspended over the years 1829–32, poised to tell us exactly why it is that the older characters like Casaubon and Bulstrode have erred and failed in their ambitions and also why the young characters such as Dorothea and Lydgate are in the process of making the mistakes that will lead them to fail. The narrator has a constant awareness of him/herself, sometimes as a scientist making "A Study of Provincial Life" (the novel's subtitle), and sometimes as an historian with an historian's knowledge of how the story ends.

For example, Dorothea's uncle and guardian Mr Brooke means well when he consents to Dorothea's marriage to Casaubon and defends his decision by predicting that Casaubon will one day enjoy the high salary of a bishop. The narrator interjects by looking forward to Brooke's future speeches as an Independent candidate for Parliament: "Mr. Brooke on this occasion little thought of the Radical speech which, at a later period, he was led to make on the incomes of the bishops" (*MM*, I:7). The narrator has knowledge both of the present event being narrated and of one that will occur in the future, both of course having already occurred in the past. It is as if the narrator had first read the novel before beginning to narrate it, for despite the fiction that the events in the novel are real, the narrator's ability to point out ironies and contradictions like this one in Brooke's politics, remind us of the textual, literary nature of this reality. Furthermore, rather than pretending to be an historian, the narrator is a commentator on the rhetorical practices of historians. In this case, the commentary on Brooke alone is not enough. The narrator must also comment on him/herself: "What elegant historian would neglect a striking opportunity for pointing out that his heroes did not foresee the history of the world or even their own actions?" (*MM*, I:7). It is such knowledge on the narrator's part, but even more the commentary on that knowledge and the search for analogies (the historian, the scientist), which shows that in *Middlemarch* Eliot's self-consciousness about her realism had reached a new level.

Later in the novel, Mr Brooke does make a speech, and the scene reveals that Eliot's attitude toward politics is even more ironic and cynical than it was in *Felix Holt*. At least Harold Transome knows that he is working against his own interests when he declares himself a Radical. When the landowning Brooke runs as an Independent – like Harold shocking his friends and neighbors – he offers a comically muddled representation of reform principles: "What do we meet for but to speak our minds – freedom of opinion, freedom of the press, liberty – that kind of thing?" (*MM*, V:51). His representation of the Reform Bill distorts and implicitly mocks it just as his effigy mocks him. In contrast to *Felix Holt*, the "mob" kills no one, but rather ridicules Brooke with a "Punch-voiced echo of his words," raises the effigy with his face "painted on a rag" and launches a "hail of eggs, chiefly aimed at the image, but occasionally hitting the original" (*MM*, V:51). Even though Brooke's political aide and the ultimate hero of the novel, Will Ladislaw, becomes an earnest politician urging reform, Mr Brooke's pro-reform speech may be seen as a humorous, ironic rewriting of Felix's "original," humorless anti-reform speech in *Felix Holt* (and in "Address to Working Men") and is an example of the heightened irony and self-awareness in *Middlemarch*.

Eliot uses the narrator's hindsight, foresight and insight to examine the mixture of external circumstances and personal choice that determines the success or failure of lives that are always solitary yet also always connected. One of the most notable failed lives in the novel is that of Mr Casaubon, whose intellectual incapacity to complete the great task of his life, the "Key to All Mythologies," and the psychological consequences of his suppressed knowledge of his incapacity, are examined in painful detail. The narrator makes overt attempts to generate sympathy for the prematurely withered scholar, but Casaubon's insensitivity to Dorothea, his jealousy and the ungenerous codicil to his will make his overall impression an unpleasant, even despicable one. Just as Eliot had protested against reviewers who misunderstood *The Mill on the Floss*, insisting that "Tom is painted with as much love and pity as Maggie" (*GEL*, III:298), so she said she sympathized with Casaubon, and there is internal as well as external evidence to suggest that she identified with his mental suffering.

The narrator, after famously interrupting the narrative by asking, "but why always Dorothea?" and turning our point of view to that of Dorothea's husband, tells us that Casaubon had "an intense consciousness within him, and was spiritually a-hungered like the rest of us" (*MM*, III:29). When Harriet Beecher Stowe asked Eliot whether Dorothea's marriage experience had been drawn from her own, Eliot denied any similarity between Lewes and Casaubon that might have been inferred from the fact that Lewes was also writing an ambitious, multi-part scholarly work, *Problems of Life and Mind*. She insisted instead on her own resemblance to the pedant: "I fear that the Casaubon-tints are not quite foreign to my own mental complexion. At any rate I am very sorry for him" (*GEL*, V:322).

The metaphor of mental complexion is a powerful one as applied especially to Lydgate, the aspiring young doctor who arrives in Middlemarch full of energy and promise but is gradually weighed down with the emotional and material cares of a bad marriage to the local beauty Rosamond Vincy. Anticipating his later temptations to gamble, the narrator remarks:

> He was at a starting-point that made a man's career a fine subject for betting, if there were any gentlemen given to that amusement who could appreciate the complicated probabilities of an arduous purpose, with all the possible thwartings and furtherings of circumstance, all the niceties of inward balance, by which a man swims and makes his point or else is carried headlong.   (*MM*, II:15)

It is precisely such "complicated probabilities" that make a life hard to predict and just such circumstances in conjunction with "inward balance" that the novel wants to examine. Lydgate is an especially risky bet because his mind, the narrator tells us in a devastating analysis of character, is "spotted with commonness" (*MM*, II:15). If we are tempted to blame Rosamond alone for thwarting Lydgate's career, the narrator reminds us that there was something about Lydgate that made him prefer Rosamond and might have undermined his career in other ways even if he had never met her. Furthermore, Lydgate's project to find the "homogeneous origin of all tissues" (*MM*, V:45) is implicitly linked with Casaubon's "Key to All Mythologies," and though admirable in intention, is similarly misguided because, as only the narrator knows, the way he put his question about primitive tissue was "not quite in the way required by the awaiting answer" (*MM*, II:15).

Through the various quests for knowledge – physiological, anthropological, and in Dorothea's case moral – Eliot explicitly raises questions about epistemology or ways of knowing. In its overall structure as well as plot details, *Middlemarch* asks its readers: what is knowledge? What can we know about the past or the future? By what means do we come to know what we can see (the natural world) and what we cannot (the insides of our minds and bodies)? Eliot had confronted this question in her work as well as in life. Casaubon's project resembles her attempt to recreate Renaissance Florence in *Romola*. Casaubon describes himself: "I live too much with the dead. My mind is something like the ghost of an ancient, wandering about the world and trying mentally to construct it as it used to be, in spite of ruin and confusing changes" (*MM*, I:2). Here Casaubon sounds both like the resuscitated Florentine in *Romola*'s Proem and like the author herself attempting to recreate the past through knowledge handed down in texts, all the while anxious about, and fearful of, failure of the sort illustrated by Casaubon. Naïve Dorothea sees only what is worthy in Casaubon's representation of his work: "To reconstruct a past world, doubtless with a view to the highest purposes of truth – what a work to be in any way present at, to assist in, though only as a lamp-holder!" (*MM*, I:2). The image connects Casaubon to Bardo, who never "effected anything but scattered work" and laments that had he succeeded he would have provided "a lamp whereby men might have studied the supreme productions of the past" (*R*, I:5).

Dorothea resembles Romola in her search for a meaningful life and some clue that will help her to see how to live. Romola grows up with the tediousness and futility of her father's scholarship, and Dorothea's marriage is a misguided attempt to acquire the knowledge that her education has denied her and that she thinks will enlighten her morally. She yearns for her life to "be filled with action at once rational and ardent; and since the time was gone by for guiding visions and spiritual directors, since prayer heightened yearning but not instruction, what lamp was there but knowledge?" (*MM*, I:10). Here the reference is to St Teresa, who found her vocation in an ardent faith and a coherent religious system and to whom Dorothea is compared in the novel's Prelude. But there seems to be an allusion to Romola also as a woman who, despite living in a time of guiding visions, tried and failed to find answers through the guidance of a "spiritual director."

Bardo amongst his fragments of antiquity, Casaubon amongst his pigeon-holed notes, and Lydgate dissecting body parts are all illustrations of why raw data needs ordering by a mind that knows what questions that data might answer. Poor Dorothea experiences this need in Rome with its "stupendous fragmentariness" (*MM*, II:20). She is too sensitive not to be impressed by the glory of Rome yet too uneducated to imagine how the historical fragments fit together. *Middlemarch* suggests that it is the human mind that interprets the sensory impressions, that gives meaning to fragments and symbols and expresses that meaning, whether in a theory like Darwin's "development hypothesis" or in a novel like *Middlemarch.*

Middlemarch's famous pier glass "parable" ostensibly applies to the egoism of Rosamond and explains how it is that Rosamond interprets every coincidence as an act of Providence designed to bring her what she wants. Introduced as a kind of experiment demonstrated to the narrator by an "eminent philosopher," the metaphor resonates throughout the novel. The pier glass "will be minutely and multitudinously scratched in all directions; but place now against it a lighted candle as a centre of illumination, and lo! the scratches will seem to arrange themselves in a fine series of concentric circles round that little sun"

(*MM*, III:27). It is, the narrator tells us, the candle that produces the "flattering illusion of concentric arrangement." So Rosamond sees Fred's illness less as a calamity for him than as an opportunity for herself because it brings Lydgate to their home. Eliot's narrator is the candle that makes the Middlemarch lives seem related when the same data observed without the narrator would seem scattered, without order or connection. The image also suggests Lydgate and Casaubon's scholarly enterprises, which are failed attempts to find order in – or impose order on – fragmentary information.

The imagery of lanterns and candles as the means by which we do or do not see is one of the many patterns that unify the novel. It is one that relates seeing to knowing as well as to the passion and energy represented by the flame. Can we be surprised that Casaubon lives at Lowick? That both Casaubon's research and his soul are benighted is illustrated through various references to light: "With his taper stuck before him he forgot the absence of windows, and in bitter manuscript remarks on other men's notions about the solar deities, he had become indifferent to sunlight" (*MM*, II:20). Mr Bulstrode, the possessor of dark secrets, turns a "moral lantern" on others that is not pleasant to the "publicans and sinners of Middlemarch" (*MM*, II:13). Scientific metaphors of telescopes and microscopes such as the "strong lens" turned on Mrs Cadwallader's match-making (*MM*, I:6) also abound. Together these images have the effect of interrogating the relationship between the seer and the seen, of questioning the notion of objectivity, while simultaneously creating a pattern or web of imagery that does the work of uniting the parts of the novel into a coherent whole.

When Will tells Dorothea that to be a poet is to have a "soul in which knowledge passes instantaneously into feeling, and feeling flashes back as a new organ of knowledge" (*MM*, II:22), and she agrees that she understands the experience, the novel is positing yet another model of knowing, one that Dorothea will learn to apply in her relations with Lydgate and Rosamond as well as with Will. It is the knowledge through feeling that her first marriage lacked and that Lydgate and Rosamond find elusive in their marriage. It is an intuitive, non-intellectual form of knowing that makes sense of other people just as science makes sense of empirical data. Dorothea, like Romola, sees only the pointless, impotent version of the intellectual life that Lydgate had found so energizing and that Eliot herself lived so passionately. Instead of holding the lamp for the producers of knowledge, Dorothea settles for a life of "unhistoric acts" that the narrator tries, with limited success, to redeem for the reader in the "Finale."

All of the primary elements of Eliot's fiction and life are present in *Middlemarch*. Chief among them is her ongoing struggle to admire and elevate the ordinary and average when she herself aspired so high above them. Most people have their spots of commonness. Some "once meant to shape their own deeds and alter the world a little" (*MM*, II:15). The tragedy of Lydgate's "coming to be shapen after the average and fit to be packed by the gross" (*MM*, II:15) lies in his giving up what he had once meant to do:

> Only those who know the supremacy of the intellectual life – the life which has a seed of ennobling thought and purpose within it – can understand the grief of one who falls from that serene activity into the absorbing soul-wasting struggle with worldly annoyances.
>
> (*MM*, VIII:73)

We can hear Eliot's voice and sympathy here for she had chosen the supremacy of the intellectual life. Dorothea and Lydgate might have been great, but historical as well as local circumstances combined with their mental complexions to determine otherwise. Caleb, Mary, and Fred would never have been great, and although theirs is the happy ending, still we must conclude that Eliot's sympathies were most fully with those who aspired to be great but failed.

The tragic idea of *Middlemarch* is expressed in the Prelude's image of the cygnet that is "reared uneasily among the ducklings in the brown pond, and never finds the living stream in fellowship with its own oary-footed kind" (*MM*, Prelude). Her next novel would be the story of a man who finds what Dorothea – the modern day St Teresa – and many other Teresas do not, "a coherent social faith and order which could perform the function of knowledge for the ardently willing soul" (*MM*, Prelude). In Judaism, Daniel Deronda discovers a coherent social faith. The fellowship he finds is of a national sort that Eliot believed was becoming increasingly important as a means of ordering experience and performing the function of knowledge in the changing world around her.

Daniel Deronda

Daniel Deronda was a daring novel to write, and probably could not have been written by any author who was not, as Eliot described herself, "independent in material things" and free from temptations to do anything other than what was "most needful to be done" (*GEL*, VI:302). Like *Romola*, *Daniel Deronda* was a research project, leading Lewes to remark of Eliot that "only learned Rabbis are so profoundly versed in Jewish history and literature as she is" (*GEL*, VI:196). The most obvious departures of Eliot's last novel are its relatively contemporary setting (October 1864 – October 1866), about a decade earlier than its publication in eight parts between February and September 1876, and its scope, encompassing the familiar English countryside, London districts from Chelsea to Holborn, and the continental travels of its characters from Frankfurt to Genoa.

Rather than recollections of a Midlands childhood or a reconstructed past world, *Daniel Deronda* reflects George Eliot's perspective on mid-nineteenth-century English society and culture – a culture so bankrupt that a vital, intelligent young woman must choose between selling herself in marriage or becoming a governess, while a handsome, intelligent young man drifts through his university education and emerges with only the vaguest sense of purpose or vocation. That Gwendolen and Daniel should cross paths while wasting time in the most depressing and demoralized of environments – a European gambling casino – suggests the lack in English culture that Eliot's novels both diagnosed and filled. An effete and dissipated cross section of European nationalities and classes, a "striking admission of human equality," the "gas-poisoned," gambling herd represents a society deaf to the drum beats of change throughout the world: the national movements in Italy and Germany, the American Civil War that is ongoing during the years of the novel's setting, and the very earliest stirrings of what would become the political and cultural movement called Zionism.

Daniel Deronda was daring in other ways. Through a plot involving adoption, illegitimacy, and ambiguities of inheritance, Eliot continued to expose the spurious nature of class distinctions based on lineal descent as she had in *Silas Marner*, *Felix Holt* and *Middlemarch*. The decaying aristocracy, represented by Grandcourt, that dissolute yet malicious "washed-out piece of cambric" (*DD*, III:36), is threatened by the upwardly mobile middle classes on the "border-territory of rank" (*DD*, I:3). The middle classes, which should be political and cultural exemplars to the nation as a whole, are materially prosperous and spiritually bankrupt. In *Daniel Deronda*, Eliot challenged complacent English Christians and Jews to see the ideal strain in Judaism as a model for preserving a coherent culture and aspiring to a national unity. Coherence of national culture to satisfy what Daniel conceives as "the imaginative need of some far-reaching relation" (*DD*, VIII:63) is Eliot's hope to regenerate rootless, secular and increasingly cosmopolitan lives.

In asking English Gentiles to take an interest in a frequently maligned minority within England, Eliot went further than ever in her attempt to generate sympathy. She wrote to Harriet Beecher Stowe: "There is nothing I should care more to do, if it were possible, than to rouse the imagination of men and women to a vision of human claims in those races of their fellow-men who most differ from them in customs and beliefs" (*GEL*, VI:301). She echoed this sentiment in writing to Blackwood, explaining that she sought to "widen the

English vision" and "let in a little conscience and refinement" (*GEL*, VI:304). In fact, in *Daniel Deronda*, she took everything further than she ever had before: the novel represents her most experimental structure, her most complex sentences, her most esoteric subjects, her most unusual metaphors, and her most ambitious moral and political vision. She seemed to be pushing the limits of the very realist novel genre she had helped to elevate as the dominant art form of the century.

For example, in *The Mill on the Floss* and *Romola*, Eliot tentatively employed a technique of representing (rather than just explaining) her characters' thoughts even as an external conversation is occurring. When Maggie and Stephen first meet, we are told that he is thinking: "I wish she would look at me again" (*Mill*, VI:2). Similarly, when Tito first meets Romola, he is thinking: "She is not really so cold and proud" (*R*, I:6). With the courtship of Gwendolen and Grandcourt, Eliot expands and develops this technique to a degree that makes it recognizable as a precursor of Modernist "stream of consciousness" narrative. She uses the "pause" in the action to make room for inner thoughts (also tried briefly in *The Mill*). It is a self-consciously experimental and distinct moment in the narrative and transforms the scene from a flirtation with ominous undertones to a psychological analysis in which Gwendolen exposes her astounding naivety and vulnerability: "(Pause, wherein Gwendolen wondered whether Grandcourt would like what she said, but assured herself that she was not going to disguise her tastes)" (*DD*, II:11). Blackwood noticed the novelty of the style, marveling that it was "like what passes through the mind after each move at a game" and that it was "as far as I know a new device in reporting a conversation" (*GEL*, VI:182).

Especially in *Middlemarch*, Eliot had balanced multiple plots and therefore needed to backtrack to narrate different strands of the plot that are occurring simultaneously. In *Daniel Deronda*, the chronology is deliberately interrupted to illustrate the epigraph with which the first chapter begins: "Men can do nothing without the make-believe of a beginning," a phrase that refers at once to the structure of the novel (which begins in the middle rather than at the beginning of the action), to Daniel's ignorance of his parental origins, and to the myths of origination that bind and define coherent groups of people like the Jews. The circularity of the narrative may be seen to reflect the larger theme of "returning" to the place of origin.

The action of the first two chapters takes place in the present. The third chapter begins a flashback to explain the circumstances in the lives of Gwendolen and Daniel leading up to their encounter in the opening scene. The flashback narrative rejoins or catches up to the original narrative in Chapter 21. The narrator tells us at the end of Chapter 20: "This was the history of Deronda, so far as he knew it, up to the time of that visit to Leubronn in which he saw Gwendolen Harleth at the gaming table" (*DD*, III:20). This provocative reference to what Daniel does not know echoes the epigraph to the chapter recalling Daniel's childhood: "Men, like planets, have both a visible and invisible history" (*DD*, II:16). Daniel's Jewish history is invisible to him, and we are asked to speculate about the life that might have been lived had circumstances differed. At the same time, we are kept in suspense by the disorienting way in which the narrative is told and by the narrator's hints at revelations to come.

Not surprisingly in a novel that holds in tension the ideas of predetermination and of chance – and which was itself an aesthetic and commercial risk – gambling plays a central role in *Daniel Deronda*.[33] Gambling is metaphoric and also literal, for the novel begins at the roulette table with no Proem (as in *Romola*), Introduction (*Felix Holt*), or Prelude (*Middlemarch*). It begins *in medias res* with the "dull gas-poisoned absorption" of the gamblers and those watching them when suddenly the moment becomes "dramatic" with the play of a young woman whose striking wins turn to striking losses after she catches the eye of the handsome young Daniel.

The famous first scene is yet another example of how *Daniel Deronda* amplifies and elaborates elements in previous novels. In *Romola*, Eliot describes the "hideous drama of the gaming-house" that could be seen in Florence's Mercato Vecchio: "the quivering eagerness, the blank despair, the sobs, the blasphemy, and the blows" (*R*, I:1). Even if Victorian gamblers at Leubronn were more refined losers than fifteenth-century Florentines, the accounts of gambling are still consistent through Eliot's works. The "hideous drama of the gaming-house" in *Romola* foreshadows the "hideous lottery" of Mrs Transome's life in *Felix Holt*.[34] And there is a similar quality in the "quivering eagerness" and "blank despair" of the Florentines and those watchers of lotteries described in *Felix Holt* as "haggard, fevered, and restless," watching for chances that yield only "blanks" (*FF*, I:1). The idea of the watcher recurs in *Middlemarch* in which Lydgate "looked on at a great deal of gambling in Paris, watching it as if it had been a disease" (*MM*, VII:66). *Daniel Deronda* begins with the view through Daniel's eyes as he watches the gambling, yet his response is more ambivalent than Lydgate's because the gambler is so beautiful. Or is she?

The opening scene of *Daniel Deronda* recalls the morally loaded language of scenes from earlier novels. As Lydgate was repulsed by "agitated fingers clutching a heap of coin" (*MM*, VII:66), so Deronda's narrator makes repulsive "the bony, yellow, crab-like hand stretching a bared wrist to clutch a heap of coin" (*DD*, I:1). Both images recall Silas Marner's fingering of his coins.

Even more than the love of money, however, seeking after thrills may be the strongest basis for Eliot's objections. Lydgate, like Mr Farebrother, is absolved morally from the sin of gambling because he tries it "not with an appetite for its excitement" but in search of money (*MM*, VII:66). In contrast, Gwendolen claims that she "cared for the excitement of play, not the winning" (*DD*, I:1), and yet the narrator assures us: "She had gone to the roulette-table not because of passion, but in search of it" (*DD*, I:2). This is a crucial insight that helps explain why, though Eliot disliked everything associated with gambling, she seemed to understand that "watching" for anticipated outcomes was a powerful human instinct. Mordecai (Ezra) Cohen watches on Blackfriars Bridge with a quality of faith no more justified rationally than that of the watchers of lotteries or roulette wheels (*DD*, V:40). He is an "eagerly expectant soul. . . . like the long-enduring watcher who at last sees the mounting signal-flame" (*DD*, VIII:63).

Daniel Deronda begins with roulette and returns to roulette in the end – this time with Eliot's only example of actual gambling "mania," what today we would call addiction. Mirah and Ezra Cohen's father is thoroughly given over to his appetite for gambling. Lapidoth has no feelings for his children and wonders only how he can obtain money from them. After his late appearance in the novel, when his children have reluctantly taken him in, he does not think about "his ireful son uttering a terrible judgment" (*DD*, VIII:66). He thinks about the roulette he used to play and how he might have played better. In his dreams, "Ezra did pass across the gaming-table, and his words were audible; but he passed like an insubstantial ghost, and his words had the heart eaten out of them by numbers and movements that seemed to make the very tissue of Lapidoth's consciousness" (*DD*, VIII:66).[35]

Ezra's words are like Lapidoth's memories of his wife, which are to him "morsels on an untasting palate, having shape and grain, but no flavour" (*DD*, VIII:62). The hollowness of Lapidoth's memories signifies the hollowness of his own heart. In his dream of the roulette table, his son is only "like an insubstantial ghost," an image which reinforces Ezra's own notion that his soul will pass into Daniel's. That transmission, however mystical, is a form of keeping memory alive, the very opposite of what Lapidoth has done in his life. If Eliot's fiction tells us anything, it is that memory is the life blood of human bonds, the "root of piety." The epigraph to *Felix Holt*'s last chapter reads: "Our Finest Hope is finest memory." Eliot expressed this sentiment throughout her life and writing, even repeating the lines in a poem called "A Minor Prophet" (1874). *Daniel Deronda* in particular explores the power of personal and collective memory, as Mordecai says to Daniel: "You shall take the inheritance; it has been gathering for ages. . . . you will take the sacred inheritance of the Jew" (*DD*, V:40).

For the *nouveau riche* clientele in Leubronn, "taking their pleasure at a higher strength," "the vice of gambling lay in losing money at it" (*DD*, I:1). But for Eliot the vice lay in winning, in the man who "sweeps within his arms the ventures of twenty chapfallen companions" (*MM*, VII:66). Throughout her fiction, as we have seen, women especially must give up ambitions and fortunes in the hope of being good. The arc of Gwendolen's career is encapsulated in the highs and lows of the roulette table when we first see her. She has soared higher (and had more money) than she might ever have expected, but by the end she has lost everything and is learning to feel, paradoxically, that losing is winning. In this she is aided by Daniel who encourages her "remorseful promptings" but counsels that, if she treats her life as a debt to be paid, she is justified in keeping Grandcourt's money. In keeping the money, however, she is free from the need to get money, and she ends the novel much as Daniel began it, with only a vague sense of wanting to be and do good. Gwendolen's masculine impulses to conquer and rule have been tamed by her experience, and just as Daniel discovers the calling that will give direction to his life, Gwendolen finds herself occupying the feminine position of resignation and renunciation.

As Eliot maintained in defense of a book which from the beginning critics have wanted to divide in two, she meant "everything in the book to be related to everything else there" (*GEL*, VI:290). An exchange between Mordecai and Mirah toward the end of the novel articulates the conflict between its idealistic and the realistic strains, specifically in terms of women. Ezra tells a story from the Midrash, somewhat reminiscent of Eliot's poem "How Lisa Loved the King," about a Jewish woman who loved a Gentile king so well that she was willing to die for his happiness:

> "She entered into prison and changed clothes with the woman who was beloved by the king, that she might deliver that woman from death by dying in her stead, and leave the king to be happy in his love which was not for her. This is the surpassing love, that loses self in the object of love."
> "No, Ezra, no," said Mirah, with low-toned intensity, "that was not it. She wanted the king when she was dead to know what she had done, and feel that she was better than the other. It was her strong self, wanting to conquer, that made her die." (*DD*, VIII:61)

In addition to revealing what we already know to be Mirah's jealousy of Gwendolen, the scene offers a rare moment in which Mirah speaks her mind and contends with her brother over the interpretation of a text and the nature of women, whom Mordecai believes are "specially framed for the love which feels possession in renouncing" (*DD*, VIII:61).

Mirah reveals that she is not merely a passive watcher. She has her own competitive instinct and desire to win, though she benefits from events that conspire to make Deronda prefer "all things unlike Gwendolen" (*DD*, VIII:63). Mordecai's paradoxical notion that women feel "possession in renouncing" is similar to what the narrator told us earlier of Gwendolen's unfeminine desire to conquer: "the desire to conquer is itself a sort of subjection" (*DD*, I:10). But it is not clear that these paradoxes hold true throughout *Daniel Deronda*.

Mirah accuses Mordecai of idealism, saying of the Midrash story, "it was not really like that," while he accuses her of having read "too many plays, where the writers delight in showing the human passions as indwelling demons" (*DD*, VIII:61). That, of course, is exactly what half of *Daniel Deronda* is about: Gwendolen's indwelling demons – "the throng of hurrying desires," as the epigraph to the novel calls them – which are manifested in her recklessness and desire to gamble with her life. The other closely interrelated half of the famously bifurcated novel is drawn to "all things unlike Gwendolen" and to what Mordecai, perhaps rightly in Eliot's opinion, describes as all too lacking in modern literature: "the relenting and devout elements of the soul" (*DD*, VIII:61).

Mordecai elevates "the surpassing love, that loses self in the object of love," whereas Mirah's opinion of the story is that "It was her strong self, wanting to conquer, that made her die." Either way, the woman dies, and having something worth dying for becomes a measure of life's worth in the novel. It is evident from *Daniel Deronda* and from her essay, "The Modern Hep! Hep! Hep!" (1879), which elaborates many of the ideas in *Daniel Deronda*, that the idealism Eliot felt might regenerate England included a belief that some things are more valuable than life itself. She feared that she was living in a society whose members saw nothing higher than self. Such a society – an empire, even a civilization – would not survive, and this is why what was "most needful to be done" (*GEL*, VI:302) was to present the English with models of idealism and to warn them of their own erosion from within. Her narrator Theophrastus explains in "The Modern Hep! Hep! Hep!" that the English know who they are: "Because there is a national life in our veins. Because there is something specifically English which we feel to be supremely worth striving for, worth dying for, rather than living to renounce it" (*TS*, 18).

Eliot made this call to the English after publishing a novel in which Judaism sufficed for an English Jew, "his judgment no longer wandering in the mazes of impartial sympathy, but choosing with that noble partiality which is man's best strength, the closer fellowship that makes sympathy practical" (*DD*, VIII:63). As she wrote in "The Modern Hep! Hep! Hep!":

Our dignity and rectitude are proportioned to our sense of relationship with something great, admirable, pregnant with high possibilities, worthy of sacrifice, a continual inspiration to self-repression and discipline by the presentation of aims larger and more attractive to our generous part than the securing of personal ease or prosperity.

(*TS*, 18)

Gwendolen may sacrifice and learn to repress her selfish desires at the end of *Daniel Deronda*, but unlike the woman in the Midrash story, and unlike many female characters in Eliot's fiction, she does not need to die. Her final promise, "I shall live," sounds a note of hope, however muted and tenuous (*DD*, VIII:69).

Impressions of Theophrastus Such

"The Modern Hep! Hep! Hep!" is the final chapter of *Impressions of Theophrastus Such*, a collection of essays and character sketches unified by theme and by the voice of a fictional author/narrator, Theophrastus. The book was rarely mentioned by Eliot or Lewes during its composition – probably in the summer and early fall of 1878 at their new country home, The Heights, Witley, in Surrey. Lewes sent the manuscript to Blackwood on 21 November 1878. It would be Eliot's last book. Lewes died on 30 November 1878, and she went into deep mourning, requesting that its publication be delayed. Finally appearing in May 1879, *Theophrastus Such* was well received, though some reviewers commented on its difficulty and unlikely prospects for popular success. It sold well, however, and only subsequently was its intellectual sophistication forgotten. Twentieth-century readers began thinking of the essays separately (if at all) and in so doing lost the challenging, experimental nature of the work as recognized by contemporary reviewers. *Theophrastus Such* has always been Eliot's least understood and appreciated book.

Because of its thematic affinity with *Daniel Deronda*, "The Modern Hep! Hep! Hep!" has often been read with that novel and quoted as if it were written in Eliot's voice. The chapter clearly expresses Eliot's views and elaborates on ideas discussed in the "Hand and Banner" chapter of *Deronda* (VI:42). It situates Mordecai's yearning for the return of the Jews to their spiritual center in a contemporary context of European nationalisms.

Reading "The Modern Hep!" as a free-standing essay does not so much distort its central arguments as overlook its rich and complicated connections to the essays that precede it, all written in the voice of Theophrastus, a narrator/author/character unique in Eliot's fiction. Theophrastus is a

nineteenth-century English man who is simultaneously a modern incarna-
tion of the ancient Greek philosopher Theophrastus (c.370–288 BC), student
of Aristotle and creator (like Eliot) of characters.[36] Knowing this makes sense
of some references in "The Modern Hep!": "An ancient Greek might not like
to be resuscitated for the sake of hearing Homer read in our universities . . ."
and: "That there is a free modern Greece is due through all infiltration of other
than Greek blood – to the presence of ancient Greece in the consciousness of
European men . . ." (*TS*, 18). In resuscitating Theophrastus, Eliot impresses this
European consciousness of ancient Greece on her readers. She also connects
the act of resuscitation to her figures for Jewish nationalism – the "new Ezras"
and "modern Maccabees" who will "steadfastly set their faces towards making
their people once more one among nations" (*TS*, 18) and who refer back to
Mordecai (Ezra) Cohen in *Deronda*. Eliot draws on the ancient Greeks and on
the Hebrew Bible to trace a joint genealogy of English culture, perhaps with
an echo of Mathew Arnold's Hellenism and Hebraism in *Culture and Anarchy*
(1869). Just as her work as a whole sought to show the "family likeness" between
her parents' generation and her own, so here her simultaneously ancient and
modern narrator embodies the animating force of the past on the present.

The second, autobiographical chapter, "Looking Backward," meditates on
the relationship of past and present, playing with the idea of time travel.
Theophrastus imagines himself living in Aristotle's time and finding it as mixed
in good and bad qualities as his own: "I gather from his disciple Theophrastus
that there were bores, ill-bred persons, and detractors even in Athens, of a
species remarkably corresponding to the English, and not yet made endurable
by being classic" (*TS*, 2). Through the voice of Theophrastus and the abun-
dance of classical and literary names given to modern characters, the past is
ever-present in these chapters about present-day English life and authorship.

The types are enduring and seem to recall characters in Eliot's novels.
Merman in "How We Encourage Research" (chapter 3) invokes the type of
petty, fruitless academic debates in which Mr Casaubon engaged. "A Half-
Breed" (chapter 9) introduces Mixtus, who is like Lydgate in making a bad
marriage that diverts him from his youthful, altruistic goals and sets him on a
path of meaningless prosperity and high standing among an anti-intellectual
social set who would never understand what he had once meant to be. The
wasted ink of Merman and the never-spilled ink of Mixtus emphasize the contemporary literary issues that run throughout the book: the social responsibility
of authorship, the acknowledgment of literary debts, and the importance of
transmitting a tradition intact to future generations. The last two chapters look
to the technological future in "Shadows of the Coming Race" (chapter 17) and
the politico-cultural future in "The Modern Hep!".

Theophrastus is both like Marian Evans Lewes – a voluntary exile from the Midlands and resident of the "nation of London" – and also like her Jewish visionary Mordecai/Ezra. The connection between Theophrastus's (and Eliot's) exile and that of the Jews becomes clear in "The Modern Hep!". What is at stake in the chapters collectively is the state of English culture, debased by the irresponsible nature of authorship and the glutted Victorian market for indiscriminate writings of all kinds. The national importance of the cultural transmission of texts is taken up in "The Modern Hep!", the title of which refers to a medieval Crusader cry that finds modern expression in anti-Jewish sentiments, which are the product of the very ignorance represented and perpetuated by the corrupt authorial practices that the book as a whole condemns.[37]

The crucial link in *Theophrastus Such*, as in *Deronda*, is between the English and the Jews. Calling himself an exile, Theophrastus reflects: "There have been many voluntary exiles in the world," including the "first exodus of the patriarchal Aryans" (*TS*, 2). By referring to "our Aryan ancestors" here and in "The Modern Hep!", he intends to invoke a past yoking European peoples together and connecting their condition of exile to the Jews, who experienced involuntary exile and dispersion from Jerusalem and underwent "the horrors of a new exile and a new dispersion" (*TS*, 18) in Medieval Europe when they were expelled from England (1209) and from Spain (1492). The antidote for this diasporic condition is the proposal that Jews attain what the English have securely and what their fellow Europeans – the nineteenth-century Greeks, Italian and Germans – were fighting for: a national center that preserves "migratory Englishmen from the worst consequences of their voluntary dispersion" (*TS*, 18). Modern English people like Theophrastus and George Eliot are becoming European, and yet because they hold the memory of their childhoods sacred and know where they came from, they are English still, even in the cosmopolitan mix of the nation of London. Theophrastus makes the case against complete assimilation for the Jews and defends their right to a modern national center to help preserve their identity wherever they may be.

Overall, *Theophrastus Such* is consistent with Eliot's belief that authorship is a moral calling, bringing responsibilities with the broadest national consequences. Scourging the failings of his contemporary would-be authors, Theophrastus argues that written texts contain within them the moral qualities of their authors and suggests that a national archive of writings that reflects the worst rather than the best in a nation can only debase the generation that inherits them. George Eliot devoted her life to filling that archive with the morally and aesthetically best writing she could produce.

Chapter 5

Afterlife

In the Victorian periodical press, it was common to publish articles, stories and poems anonymously or under a pseudonym. For example, Lewes wrote theatre reviews for the *Leader* under the name "Vivian," and Eliot's essays in the *Westminster Review* were published anonymously. While insiders often knew the identities of anonymous authors, the practice allowed readers to judge contributions objectively and gave the impression of a journal speaking in one voice. On the other hand, original work might go unacknowledged unless – as George Eliot found – the veil of anonymity was lifted.

When Marian Evans Lewes published "The Sad Fortunes of the Reverend Amos Barton" anonymously in *Blackwood's Magazine* (Jan.–Feb. 1857), she had an additional reason for not wanting to advertise her name. Mrs Lewes was not her real (or at least not her legal) name. It was a fiction, but one that – unlike George Eliot – might distract or put off readers by calling attention to her unmarried status. So when she published *Scenes of Clerical Life* as a book (1858), she employed the pseudonym George Eliot partly for personal reasons and also to see what kind of response her writing would receive without preconceptions based on her identity or her gender. The strategy worked in that *Scenes* and her next book *Adam Bede* (1859) established the reputation of George Eliot so completely that even questions about the domestic life of Marian Evans Lewes could not undermine it. After she was compelled to reveal her authorship to prevent the imposter Joseph Liggins from taking the credit for her work, Marian Evans Lewes continued to publish under the name George Eliot.

Consequently the name George Eliot acquired influence, and she used it for all her major publications. Some works originally appearing unsigned in journals, such as "The Lifted Veil" and "Brother Jacob," later appeared in the Cabinet Edition of her complete works (20 vols., 1878–80). In another experiment, she published four essays under the pseudonym "Saccharissa" in the *Pall Mall Gazette* (1865). The draw of the name George Eliot is evident in George Smith's offer of £10,000 to serialize the as-yet-unwritten *Romola* in the *Cornhill Magazine* (27 February 1862), as well as in the sale of poems such as

"The Legend of Jubal" (1870) and "Armgart" (1871) to *Macmillan's Magazine* and the *Atlantic Monthly* in the US, even though she was not known as a poet. As Donald Gray observes: "One of the most remarkable signs of Eliot's eminence is that her name could sell poetry."[1]

The branding of the name George Eliot began with her approval of Alexander Main's *Wise, Witty and Tender Sayings in Prose and Verse selected from the work of George Eliot* (1871). Written the year Main's *The George Eliot Birthday Book* (1878) appeared, the chapter of *Theophrastus Such* entitled "The Wasp Credited with the Honeycomb," betrayed her cynicism about the cache of names. Theophrastus insists: "for, check ourselves as we will, the first impression of any sort of work must depend on a previous attitude of mind, and this will constantly be determined by the influences of a name" (*TS*, 11). Theophrastus complains that people are too incompetent or insecure to judge a work blindly and instead use "names as guides in criticism."

Main, a Scotsman with minor literary ambitions, was a passionate admirer and flatterer of Eliot. Blackwood nicknamed him "the Gusher." Main's books capitalized on the penchant, especially among Victorian women, for transcribing extracts from favorite books. He selected and reproduced passages from Eliot's novels in such a way that the name George Eliot represented not just the author of the books but their unifying subject matter. Taken out of their original contexts, these "sayings" had value only because George Eliot said them. Leah Price's *The Anthology and the Rise of the Novel* (2000) examines the phenomenon of publishing sections of works out of context, or rather in a new context of juxtaposition with other excerpts. Beginning with the novels of Samuel Richardson, she provides a history of such anthologizing including a case study of Main's extracts from Eliot's writing. Price's work represents recent interest in the history of the book, a kind of cultural studies that shows us how publishing and marketing affected the form and content of Victorian literature. Other contributions to our knowledge about Eliot and publishing history include Carol Martin's *George Eliot's Serial Fiction* (1994), which establishes the historical details of Eliot's serial and part publications and David Finkelstein's *The House of Blackwood: Author–Publisher Relations in the Victorian Era* (2002), which situates Eliot's long and profitable relationship with her publisher in the broader context of author–publisher relations.

According to Alexander Welsh, the value and currency of a public name and reputation emerged during the nineteenth century. Consequently, a good name could be damaged. The concept of blackmail developed as a crime that traded on the value of reputation. In *George Eliot and Blackmail* (1985), Welsh provides extensive cultural explanation for Eliot's fictional blackmailers, such as Dunsey Cass, David Faux, Maurice Christian, and John Raffles, as well as the psychological manipulation by Grandcourt, whose secret (Lydia Glasher), becomes a means of controlling Gwendolen, its revelation being more damaging to her than to him. Exploring the production and dissemination of knowledge in the print media, constructions of public reputations with monetary value, and the creation of a right to privacy, Welsh reads Eliot's blackmailing characters in relation to the secret of her authorial identity and the open secret of her "marriage" to Lewes.

In "Liszt, Wagner and Weimar" (1855), Eliot writes that, in contrast to musical and dramatic performers, "the genius who can leave permanent creation behind him knows that he shall live for the next age more emphatically than for his own" (*SCW*, p. 83). She continues: "Fame is but another word for the sympathy of mankind with individual genius" (*SCW*, p. 83). Her poem, "The Legend of Jubal" (1870), ends with the inventor of music being consoled by an angel after his miserable death. The consolation is that he has left behind something that can never die:

> It is the glory of the heritage
> Thy life has left, that makes thy outcast age:
> Thy limbs shall lie dark, tombless on this sod,
> Because thou shinest in man's soul, a god,
> Who found and gave new passion and new joy
> That nought but Earth's destruction can destroy.
>
> (*Poetry* I, lines 774–779)

At this time, following Thornie Lewes's death, Eliot seemed particularly preoccupied with what artists leave behind when they die.

Her specific awareness of posterity's judgment is evident in her concern about Lewes's reputation. After his death in 1878, she devoted herself to finishing his five-volume *Problems of Life and Mind,* which she did in 1879. She watched anxiously for appraisals of his scientific contributions in obituaries and reviews. Critics have noted the irony of Eliot finishing Lewes's ambitious work after his death considering that this is precisely what Dorothea refused to do in *Middlemarch* after Casaubon dies, leaving his "Key to All Mythologies" in fragments. In contrast to her fictional widow, however, Eliot was convinced of Lewes's importance as a scientific thinker and was determined to see his work acknowledged. K. K. Collins and Martha Vogler have discussed this aspect of Eliot's life and her concern with posterity in particularly interesting and focused biographical essays.[2] Even if Lewes's fame would never equal hers, she wanted him to be appreciated, to have that "sympathy of mankind with individual genius" – or at least the respect of his scientific peers.

Inevitably, Eliot also worried about her posthumous reputation and the afterlife of her work. This is perhaps why she attempted to control the flow of information about her life. When she died in 1880, her letters from Lewes were buried with her. She had married the much younger John Cross knowing that he would survive her, and she authorized him to publish extracts from her letters and journals. Even before Cross could complete his book, Mathilde Blind published the first biography, *George Eliot* (1883), based on interviews with friends such as the Brays. But Blind did not have the privileged access to letters, diaries, and family members that Cross enjoyed as the widower. With *George Eliot's Life as Related in her Letters and Journals* (1885), he produced the kind of biography he thought his wife would have wanted. He also had the advantage of having known her for years and, as her husband, of knowing her wishes about her future biographies. The sanitized version of her life that he produced was a concession to the public, as well as a pre-emption of unauthorized biographies that might be eager to exploit the past scandal of her relationship with Lewes.

Reviewers had little sympathy with the humorless moral paragon Cross created by heavily editing the documentary remains of a life that was in fact full of unconventional acts: moving to London alone, editing a radical journal, living with a married man, and publishing best-sellers under a man's name. William Gladstone famously called the *Life* a "Reticence in 3 volumes" (*GEL*, I:xiv). Many readers were disappointed with the book, which only confirmed their late-Victorian notion of Eliot as a "sibyl." Henry James's sister Alice James, though she admired Eliot's novels, confided to her diary that the *Life* was "a monument of ponderous dreariness" that gave her the "impression, morally and physically, of mildew."[3]

In the years following her death, Eliot's reputation inevitably suffered in a changing moral and aesthetic climate that was producing real and fictional "New Women" – early feminists who spoke out and stepped out into the pubic sphere, shocking an older generation of Victorians – as well as proponents of "Art for Art's Sake" – aesthetes like Oscar Wilde opposed to the moral seriousness of Victorian literature and asserting beauty as the only goal of art. To this new generation, Eliot was an unfashionable repressed Victorian. After some important works of retrospective appraisal such as Leslie Stephen's *George Eliot* (1902), published the year after Queen Victoria's death and twenty two years after Eliot's, her name was no longer influential. Reviewing Stephen's book, the American novelist Edith Wharton referred to Eliot's "momentary neglect" as one of the "interlunar phases" that was "the lot of all great writers."[4] Wharton defended particularly Eliot's use of science and seemed to sympathize with her as an intellectually ambitious woman born too soon. As less highbrow early twentieth-century publications suggest, Eliot never faded completely from memory. In *The True Story of George Eliot* (1905), for example, William Mottram, a distant relative of the Evans family, gives a positive spin to the idea that Eliot was a "preacher" – a role about which other critics complained – and asserts her continued influence: "No author is more written about than George Eliot."[5]

One stubborn late Victorian perception was that Eliot's best work was to be found in her early novels and that her powers went into decline with *Romola*. In *The Makers of English Fiction* (1905), W. J. Dawson asserts: "*Romola* marks her decadence . . . in *Middlemarch* this decadence is still more pronounced, and it is complete in the utterly tedious *Daniel Deronda*."[6] The use of the term "decadence" is particularly interesting as it allies Eliot with the *fin de siècle*, amoral Decadent movement, which was a reaction against the realist, moral literature she epitomized.

Turn-of-the-century readers seem not to have understood what some of her most perceptive contemporaries did: the experimental style, complex inter-action of ideas, and layers of resonant allusions. This movement away from a more straightforward, accessible and realist representational style toward more intellectually dense and allusive prose may be what Dawson calls "decadent," and it is intriguing to think of Eliot's late work as merging with that of the late nineteenth-century Decadents as a precursor to Modernism, rather than strictly as mid-nineteenth-century realism. Such a realigned literary genealogy is supported when we consider that, as her career progressed, Eliot became less interested in pleasing the majority of readers, more defiant, and even disdainful of popular tastes.[7]

In 1919, the centenary of Eliot's birth, Virginia Woolf went against the tide of critical thought at the time, attempting to recuperate the vitality of Eliot's life and intellect from the dulling effect of Cross's *Life* and defending her late novels. She proclaimed that *Middlemarch* was one of the few English novels written for "grown-up people."[8] Joan Bennett, who contributed to the mid-twentieth-century revival of interest in Eliot's work, agreed with Woolf and argued that this sense of maturity resulted because "unlike many of her contemporaries, she was not distracted from the contemplation of her subject by the wish to provide the sort of entertainment the reader demanded."[9] Eliot became less interested in entertaining as she became more serious about her art and as her notion of what constituted art developed in conjunction with her public persona as a literary genius and national icon.

The assessment of the late novels is quite different today, and that change began with the critical efforts of Bennett and F. R. Leavis. Bennett argued that "it is the later works that appeal to us especially."[10] In *The Great Tradition* (1948), Leavis highlighted aspects of *Felix Holt* and *Middlemarch*, but devoted most of his discussion to *Daniel Deronda,* whose qualities emerge favorably by contrast to Henry James's *Portrait of a Lady* (1881), which Leavis demonstrates is indebted to *Deronda.* It is an odd and divisive argument, however, in that its praise is reserved for the Gwendolen "part" of the novel. In a complex and provocative move, he suggests that Gwenolen's story would make a superior novel if the part about Deronda were eliminated, a position that has left subsequent critics the job of proving Eliot's assertion that everything in the novel is related to everything else. Claudia Johnson has examined the socio-cultural contexts of Leavis's decision to exclude the Jewish part of *Deronda.*[11]

While Leavis was helping to transform Eliot studies by applying new critical standards and methods, Gordon S. Haight was collecting her letters, which he published, along with excerpts from her journals, and from the letters of Lewes, Blackwood, and others in the seven-volume *George Eliot Letters* (1954–5). Biographies up to this time still relied heavily on Cross. Mary Deakin's *The Early Life of George Eliot* (1913), Anna Kitchell's *George Lewes and George Eliot: A Review of Records* (1932), and Blanche Colton Williams's *George Eliot: A Biography* (1936) should be credited as important contributions that pre-dated the publication of the letters. In *State of the Art: George Eliot, a guide through the critical maze* (1990), Graham Handley provides accounts and assessments of these and other lesser known works. Haight's edition of the letters and the biography he wrote using them, *George Eliot: A Biography* (1968), are the foundation of subsequent studies that take biography into account or that look to her letters for interpretive clues to her fiction.

Rosemarie Bodenheimer's innovative study, *The Real Life of Mary Ann Evans* (1994), provides theoretically informed close readings of the letters to shed new light on the relationship between Eliot's life and writing. Additionally, biographies have been offered by Frederick Karl (1995) and Katherine Hughes (1999). Rosemary Ashton's *George Eliot: A Life* (1996) complements her *G. H. Lewes: A Life* (1991), the definitive biography of Lewes, full of new information which was supplemented by William Baker's three volume edition of the *Letters of George Henry Lewes* (1995/1999).

Other documents important to understanding Eliot's life include John Chapman's diaries, which Haight published in *George Eliot and John Chapman* (1940). Two more volumes of *The George Eliot Letters* (Vols. 8–9, 1978) include many extracts from an unpublished manuscript written by Eliot's devoted admirer Edith Simcox called "The Autobiography of a Shirtmaker." K. A. McKenzie published *Edith Simcox and George Eliot* (1961) and a complete edition of Simcox's extraordinary work was published as *A Monument to the Memory of George Eliot: Edith Simcox's Autobiography of a Shirtmaker,* edited by Constance M. Fulmer and Margaret Barfield (1998). Supplementing the letters, we also have *The Journals of George Eliot* (eds. Margaret Harris and Judith Johnstone, 1998). Much of the critical work being done today depends upon such scholarly contributions.

The question of how Eliot was critically received is different from that of how she influenced a later generation of writers. Writing on the centenary of her death, Elaine Showalter discusses her influence on a century of women writers. "The Greening of Sister George" (1980) begins by considering the difficulties experienced by authors writing in the shadow of Eliot's fame, such as Margaret Oliphant, Eliza Lynn Linton, Mary Elizabeth Braddon, Elizabeth Robins, and Dinah Mulock Craik: "Eliot's unquestioned ascendancy as a fictional realist and moralist defined the boundaries of aspiration for the women forced into secondary status in relation to her."[12] At the same time, we should remember that her philosophical seriousness influenced Henry James, her treatment of the past influenced Marcel Proust, and her focus on women had its impact on major female authors such as Edith Wharton and Virginia Woolf. Clearly, the diffusive influence of her novels on other novelists in the generation following her death was greater than the critical attention paid to them.

Interest in Eliot's work today is more academic than popular. Editions of her work remain in print, and a BBC television mini-series of *Middlemarch* (1994) brought brief popular attention to the novel. Yet, her popularity outside of the classroom and academic discourse does not compare to that of Jane Austen and Charles Dickens. There are no commercial successes to rival Emma Thompson's film adaptation of *Sense and Sensibility* (1995) or the film version of *Emma* starring Gwyneth Paltrow (1996). Eliot wrote no eternal holiday classic like *A Christmas Carol*.

Critical attention is another matter. Two journals, the *George Eliot Review* in the UK and *George Eliot–G. H. Lewes Studies* in the US, publish specialized articles about Eliot and Lewes as well as newly discovered letters and notebooks. Companions have been published: the encyclopedic *Oxford Reader's Companion to George Eliot* (ed. John Rignall, 2000) is an invaluable resource, and the *Cambridge Companion to George Eliot* (ed. George Levine, 2001) offers original essays by various critics on broad topics such as Eliot and religion, philosophy, science, politics, publishing and gender. While aimed more at students and scholars than general readers, these companions would be useful to anyone interested in Eliot's works.

The history of George Eliot criticism is the history of literary criticism generally and it is worth reviewing approaches to her work since Leavis's *The Great Tradition* and Haight's edition of the letters provided the foundations for Eliot scholarship and criticism. Literary criticism (as opposed to reviewing on the one hand and biography on the other) emerged in force only after World War I.

In *Literary Theory: An Introduction* (1983), Terry Eagleton surveys the history of English literature's institutionalization in England: "English literature rode to power on the back of wartime nationalism; but it also represented a search for spiritual solutions on the part of an English ruling class whose sense of identity had been profoundly shaken."[13] He includes an examination of the politics of F. R. and Q. D. Leavis and the journal *Scrutiny* (1932–53), founded to implement the rigorous critical practice needed to judge and canonize the best of literature in English in the belief that great art could provide an antidote to an increasingly industrialized, commercialized society and stand as a bulwark against the onslaught of mass culture. In this sense, Eliot's critical neglect and her recovery, to which F. R. Leavis was so central, has as much to do with developments in the way criticism was practiced as it does with characteristics intrinsic to her work.

The second half of the twentieth century has seen the rise of Eliot's reputation and has brought extensive attention to her work, as well as interestingly hostile reactions. The elevation and the attacks have come from both sides of the Atlantic, but in general what were seen as weaknesses by Victorian critics have been recognized by a post-Modernist generation as artistic strengths.

After Leavis and Bennett called attention to the mastery and modernity of the late fiction, the next methodologically innovative critical approach to Eliot's accomplishments came with the New Critical principles of close reading and formal analysis. In *The Novels of George Eliot* (1959), Barbara Hardy argued against a tradition dating back to Henry James, which held Eliot's multi-plot novels to be formless. In contrast, Hardy argued that the "form of the novel can mean the co-operation of a large number of forms within the novel."[14]

The 1970s saw the setting of interest in formalism and the rise of more explicitly political criticism. The concerns of feminist critics provided a new way of looking at Eliot's female characters and at her own achievements. While feminist criticism called attention to Eliot's fiction, the critics themselves were often disappointed with the fates of heroines like Maggie and Dorothea and lamented Eliot's failure to give readers then and now examples of strong, successful women like herself.[15]

Marxist critics like Raymond Williams and Terry Eagleton were unconvinced that she was extending sympathy to the disenfranchised classes. The critique of Eliot was part of a larger critique of nineteenth-century Realism. Eliot's point of view and values were too conservative and bourgeois, reinforcing the status quo and failing to promote social change. In *Social Figures: George Eliot, Social History, and Literary Representation* (1987), Daniel Cottom builds on the work of the Marxist critics Georg Lukacs and Raymond Williams to interrogate the "myth" of the liberal intellectual in Eliot's work, as well as various other myths perpetuated by realist fiction. In his introduction to that work, Terry Eagleton writes: "That configuration of sympathies which is the realist novel is itself the effect of a whole cluster of disciplinary techniques and pedagogical devices, constructing in its readers the very appropriate forms of subjective inwardness it disinterestedly purports to examine in its characters."[16]

Leavis's work was engaged in a cultural politics of creating a national canon of the best that has been thought and written, in the tradition of Matthew Arnold. Rather than evaluating the quality of her work as Leavis did, the trend has been to evaluate her politics. Inevitably, she has been found not feminist, socialist, or anti-racist enough for the post-1960s academic left. But even her harshest critics continue to take her and her work seriously for its importance to our understanding of nineteenth-century culture and society. The force of her intellect and complexity of her fiction have been irresistible to increasingly theoretical critics of language, psychology, and cultural dynamics.

In the 1980s, critics practicing the critical methodology known as "deconstruction," strongly influenced by the work of Jacques Derrida, took an interest in Eliot's fiction. In his reading of *The Mill on the Floss*, J. Hillis Miller explains:

> ... 'deconstruction' is not something that the reader does to a text; it is something that the text does to itself. The text then does something to the reader as she or he is led to recognize the possibility of two or more rigorously defensible, equally justifiable, but logically incompatible readings of the text in question.[17]

The school of criticism known as New Historicism, influenced by the work of Michel Foucault, found new ways to contextualize Eliot's work, such as Catherine Gallagher's analysis of *Felix Holt* in *The Industrial Reformation of English Fiction* (1980). Critics who sought to historicize and attend to language outside of any defined critical movement paid special attention to Eliot's relationship to science, including Gillian Beer's *Darwin's Plots* (1983), a methodologically distinctive intertextual analysis of Darwinian language in the works of Eliot and Thomas Hardy.

Interest in Eliot's work is greater than ever. Recent critics have been interested in the way she speaks to issues of class, gender, race, and national identity, especially in *Daniel Deronda* and *Impressions of Theophrastus Such*. Entire books have been devoted to Eliot and Judaism, race, empire, and national identity. Debates have been ongoing, especially about *Daniel Deronda*, and critics have argued about the proto-Zionist politics of the novel as well as about the unlikely question of whether or not Daniel was circumcised.

General introductions by Gillian Beer (1986), Jennifer Uglow (1987), and Kristin Brady (1992) focus on "the Woman Question" and on Eliot's feminism, chipping away at some of Haight's dated biases, such as the notion that Eliot was not suited to "stand alone" and needed "someone to lean on." Even though Eve Sedgwick devoted a chapter to homosociality in *Adam Bede* in her groundbreaking book *Between Men* (1985), little work has been done on Eliot from within Queer studies. One exception is Jacob Press's "Same-Sex Unions in Modern Europe: *Daniel Deronda* Altneuland, and the Homoerotics of Jewish Nationalism" in Sedgwick's collection *Novel Gazing* (1997).

One of the first responses to Eliot's English stories was to try to find "originals" for them, sometimes taking a literal and naïve perspective on the fiction-writing process. Eliot admitted that Mr Tryan and the Dempsters in "Janet's Repentance" were portraits of Nuneaton residents recollected from her school days, but would not admit to other portraits (rather just suggestions, such as the Revd John Gwyther for Amos, her father for Adam Bede, Mary Voce for Hetty and Elizabeth Evans for Dinah Morris).

Finding originals has never been a precise or sophisticated form of criticism. What would it really mean to have an "original" for a character since the attempt of any person to represent the inner life of another is of necessity a fiction? Eliot was both defensive and sarcastic about people claiming originals. Speaking of her first book, she told Blackwood: "We are all apt to forget how little there is about us that is unique, and how very strongly we resemble many other insignificant people who have lived before us" (*GEL*, II:376). Her last book, *Theophrastus Such*, is an exercise in deconstructing the idea of originals and originality. Is the ancient Greek philosopher Theophrastus an "original" for the contemporary Londoner? Is Theophrastus Such an imitation? A copy? Or, someone completely original who happens to share a name with his ancient counterpart?

And yet, the idea of identifying originals has persisted well beyond the 1850s when "keys" to her characters were circulated in Nuneaton. One example is a collection reprinting essays by Gordon Haight, *George Eliot's Originals and Contemporaries* (ed. Hugh Whittemeyer, 1992). Some critics have tried to develop more inclusive "fusion" theories in which not one but several originals are identified. In *George Eliot's English Travels* (2005), Kathleen McCormack argues that Eliot's character constructions were not "one-to-one renderings of people she knew, but composites" that may be described as "literary pointillism, assemblages of small units that, when viewed from a proper distance combine to yield representations of landscapes and figures."[18] In a similarly complex model articulated in *George Eliot: A Critic's Biography* (2006), Barbara Hardy contends that fiction's "particularities come out of a process in which real lives are abstracted and re-particularized." *Middlemarch* is not "disguised autobiography or portraiture, but an imaginative recomposition, concentrated and diffuse, direct and indirect, public and private, psychological, social and moral."[19]

The ambiguity that arises from this approach is evident in the fact that McCormack makes the case for Georgiana Burne-Jones as a model for Dorothea (chapter 7), while Hardy makes the case for Jane Senior (chapter 4). According to the composite theory, both could be right. Whereas McCormack uses pointillism as an analogy, A. D. Nuttall, in *Dead from the Waist Down: Scholars and Scholarship in Literature and the Popular Imagination* (2003), uses Francis Galton's nineteenth-century composite photographs to explain the multiple originals comprising Mr Casaubon including the sixteenth-century scholar Isaac Casaubon and his Victorian biographer Mark Pattison.

This question of identifying originals brings us back to the influence of a name. Eliot's complex relationship to her own names is reflected in the double identity of David Faux in "Brother Jacob," the proliferation and confusion of names in *Felix Holt* (Transome, Trounsem), the double name of Mordecai/Ezra Cohen, and Daniel Deronda's reference to himself as "the so-called Deronda" (*DD*, VII:50), as if somewhere his real name existed if only he knew where to find it. In her real life, George Eliot chose to be – not Marian, or even Mary Anne Evans – but Mrs Lewes. Critical preoccupation with the morality of her relationship with Lewes has obscured the fact that she made a fiction into a reality. George Eliot was a pen name, but it endures on her tombstone and in the titles of her biographies from Cross to today. She was a character in her own life, with multiple names, a conflicted identity, and an insistence that what was fictional was true. Perhaps the power of an imagination that transformed the fiction of her marriage into a reality in her life is the reason that her fiction still seems so real to us.

Notes

1 Life

1. *George Eliot's Life as related in her Letters and Journals.* Arranged and edited by her husband, J. W. Cross. 3 vols. (New York: Harper Brothers, 1885), I:113.
2. Rosemarie Bodenheimer, "A woman of many names," *The Cambridge Companion to George Eliot*, ed. George Levine (Cambridge: Cambridge University Press, 2001), p. 26.
3. The meeting is described by Rosemary Ashton in *George Eliot: A Life* (London: Hamish Hamilton, 1996), p. 1.
4. Ashton, *George Eliot*, p. 104.
5. *The Journals of George Eliot*, ed. Margaret Harris and Judith Johnston (Cambridge: Cambridge University Press, 1996).
6. *George Eliot: The Critical Heritage*, ed. David Carroll (London: Routledge & Kegan Paul, 1971), p. 332.

2 Historical contexts

1. Edmund Burke, *Reflections on the Revolution in France*, ed. L. G. Mitchell (Oxford: Oxford University Press, 1999), p. 33.
2. Quoted in John M. Picker, *Victorian Soundscapes* (Oxford: Oxford University Press, 2003), p. 109.
3. Matthew Arnold, *Culture and Anarchy*, ed. Jane Garnett (Oxford: Oxford University Press, 2006), p. 53.

3 Literary influences

1. John Rignall notes that she first read the *Poetics* in 1857 and reread it in 1865 and 1873. See "Aristotle," *The Oxford Reader's Companion to George Eliot*, ed. John Rignall (Oxford: Oxford University Press, 2000).
2. Aristotle, *Poetics* in *Introduction to Aristotle*, ed. Richard McKeon (New York: Random House, 1947), Ch. 21. Hereafter cited in the text.

3. See A. G. van den Broek, "Shakespeare at the Heart of George Eliot's England," *George Eliot–G. H. Lewes Studies* 24–25, no. 2 (1993 Sept): 36–64, p. 36.
4. See Margaret Anne Doody, "George Eliot and the Eighteenth-century Novel," *Nineteenth Century Fiction* 35 (1980–81): 260–91.
5. Eliot and Lewes read *Mansfield Park* aloud in 1874.
6. William Wordsworth and Samuel Taylor Coleridge, *Lyrical Ballads and Related Writings*, ed. William Richey and Daniel Robinson (Boston: Houghton Mifflin, 2002), p. 396.

4 Works

1. The publication of Lewes's second series of *Seaside Studies* (June–October 1857) coincided with the appearance of Eliot's third scene, "Janet's Repentance."
2. Eliot read *Mansfield Park* in December of 1856, the same month she began "Mr. Gilfil's Love Story."
3. Neil Hertz has connected the drop of ink with the dark pool, suggesting that both are instances of Eliot's "thematizing of the operations of the novelist." See *George Eliot's Pulse* (Stanford: Stanford University Press, 2003), p. 97.
4. She changed this description to "a patient, prolific, loving-hearted woman."
5. Gordon Haight, *George Eliot: A Biography* (Oxford: Oxford University Press, 1968), p. 279.
6. G. H. Lewes, *The Biographical History of Philosophy, From its Origins in Greece down to the Present Day* (London: John W. Parker and Sons, 1857), p. 4.
7. Ibid., p. 5–6.
8. *George Eliot: The Critical Heritage*, ed. David Carroll (London: Routledge and Kegan Paul, 1971), p. 135.
9. *George Eliot: Critical Assessments*, 3 vols., ed. Stuart Hutchinson (East Sussex: Helm Information Ltd, 1996), II, p. 18.
10. Mary Poovey, "Writing about Finance in Victorian England: Disclosure and Secrecy in the Culture of Investment," *Victorian Studies* 45:1 (Autumn 2002), p. 36.
11. These three works were published together in one volume of the Cabinet Edition of Eliot's works in 1878.
12. Jonathan Swift, *Gulliver's Travels*, ed. Paul Turner (Oxford: Oxford University Press, 1986), III, 10.
13. *Ibid.*, III, 10.
14. See Kate Flint, "Blood, Bodies, and the Lifted Veil," *Nineteenth-Century Literature* 51, no. 4 (March 1997): 455–73.
15. See Susan De Sola Rodstein, "Sweetness and Dark: George Eliot's 'Brother Jacob,'" *Modern Language Quarterly* 52:3 (1991): 295–317.
16. "Nemesis is the goddess of retribution or vengeance, who reverses excessive good fortune, checks presumption, and punishes wrongdoing; (hence) a person who

or thing which avenges, punishes, or brings about someone's downfall; an agent of retribution" (*Oxford English Dictionary*).

17. The original £10,000 had been offered for sixteen parts. Eliot negotiated instead twelve parts for £7,000. In the end, she needed fourteen parts to finish the novel but was not paid any more for the additional two.

18. *Romola*, ed. Andrew Brown (Oxford: World's Classics, 1994), p. 549

19. She began making notes in May of 1861 and continued researching until she began writing on New Year's Day, 1862.

20. George Eliot, *The Journals of George Eliot* (17–19 February 1862).

21. See Hilary Fraser, *The Victorians and Renaissance Italy* (Oxford: Blackwell, 1992). For the modern context, see Maura O'Connor, *The Romance of Italy and the English Political Imagination* (New York: St. Martin's, 1998).

22. Cross, *George Eliot's Life*, II:352.

23. "Felix Holt," *Oxford Reader's Companion to George Eliot*, p. 116.

24. For a history of the poetry's reception, see the introduction to *The Complete Shorter Poetry of George Eliot* (2 vols), ed. Antonie Gerard van den Broek (London: Pickering and Chatto, 2005).

25. In the introduction to her unpublished edition of Eliot's poetry (1969), Cynthia Ann Secor speculated that Eliot wanted to "achieve poetic stature of the kind described in Shelley's *A Defence of Poetry*" (quoted in *Complete Shorter Poetry*, I:xxix).

26. Dates refer to the year of publication, which sometimes differs from the year of composition.

27. Bodenheimer, *The Real Life*, p. 182.

28. George Eliot, *Poems*, Vol. II (Boston: Dana Estes & Co. Arbury Edition, n.d.), Bk. 5.

29. *The Journals of George Eliot* (19, 20, 21 February 1865).

30. See Martin Bidney, "'The Legend of Jubal' as Romanticism Refashioned: Struggles of a Spirit in George Eliot's Musical Midrash," *George Eliot–G. H. Lewes Studies* (2007).

31. "Agatha" (January 1869), "How Lisa Loved the King" (February 1869), "Brother and Sister" (July 1869), "The Legend of Jubal" (January 1870) and "Armgart" (August 1870). Dates refer to completion rather than publication.

32. *The Journals of George Eliot* (31 December 1870).

33. See Wilfred Stone, "The Play of Chance and Ego in *Daniel Deronda*," *Nineteenth-Century Literature* 58:1 (June 1998): 25–55.

34. In letters describing the incident in Homburg that inspired the opening scene of *Deronda*, Eliot refers to the "hateful, hideous women staring at the board like stupid monomaniacs" (*GEL*, V:312) and to the "monstrous hideousness" of the casino (*GEL*, V:314). According to the *OED*, "hideous" originally meant "causing dread or horror"; this has gradually passed into "revolting to the senses or feelings." The older sense of causing dread or horror runs through *Deronda*, as in the panel with the painting of the dead face.

35. For a reading of this image, see Neil Hertz, *George Eliot's Pulse* (Ch. 8).
36. Theophrastus's *Characters*, composed of thirty sketches of "types" observed in the city of Athens, initiated its own form and tradition. Translated into Latin in 1592 by Isaac Casaubon, it became a model for a kind of formulaic character-writing popular in Europe as late as the early nineteenth century. Eliot read Casaubon's translation in Geneva and she was familiar with the French writer Jean de La Bruyere's French translation, *Caractères de Théophraste, traduit du grec, avec les Caractères ou le Mouers de ce Siècle* (1688).
37. See Nancy Henry, "Ante-Anti-Semitism: George Eliot's *Impressions of Theophrastus Such*," *Victorian Identities: Social and Cultural Formations in Nineteenth-Century Literature*, ed. Ruth Robbins and Julian Wolfreys (New York: St. Martin's Press, 1996).

5   Afterlife

1. Donald Gray, "George Eliot and her Publishers," *Cambridge Companion*, p. 194.
2. K. K. Collins, "Reading George Eliot Reading Lewes's Obituaries," *Modern Philology* (November 1987): 153–69; Martha Vogeler, "George Eliot as Literary Widow," *Huntington Library Quarterly* (Spring 1988): 73–87.
3. Quoted in Bodenheimer, *Real Life*, p. 1.
4. Edith Wharton, "A Review of Leslie Stephen," *Bookman* (London, XV, May 1902), p. 247. Reprinted in *George Eliot: Critical Assessments*, Vol. III, ed. Stuart Hutchinson (East Sussex: Helm Information Ltd, 1996), p. 53.
5. William Mottram, *The True Story of George Eliot* (London: Francis Griffiths, 1905).
6. Quoted in Joan Bennett, *George Eliot: Her Mind and Her Art* (Cambridge: Cambridge University Press, 1948), p. x.
7. See K. M. Newton, "George Eliot as Proto-Modernist," *Cambridge Quarterly* 27, no. 4 (1998): 275–86.
8. *TLS* (20 November 1919): 657–8.
9. Bennett, *George Eliot*, p. xi.
10. Bennett, *George Eliot*, p. xi.
11. See Claudia L. Johnson, "F. R. Leavis and 'The Great Tradition' of the English Novel and the Jewish Part," *Nineteenth Century Literature* 56:2: 198–227.
12. Elaine Showalter, "The Greening of Sister George," *Nineteenth Century Fiction* 35 (December 1980): 292–311. Reprinted in Hutchinson, Vol. 4, p. 139.
13. Terry Eagleton, *Literary Theory: An Introduction* (Minneapolis: University of Minnesota Press, 1983), p. 30.
14. Barbara Hardy, *The Novels of George Eliot* (London: Athlone Press, 1959), p. 5.
15. See Zelda Austen, "Why Feminist Critics are Angry with George Eliot," *College English* 37, no. 6 (1976): 549–61.

16. Daniel Cottom, *Social Figures: George Eliot, Social History and Literary Representation*, introduction by Terry Eagleton (Minneapolis: University of Minnesota Press, 1987), p. xvi.

17. J. Hillis Miller, "The Two Rhetorics: George Eliot's Bestiary," *Writing and Reading Differently: Deconstruction and the Teaching of Composition and Literature*, ed. G. Douglas Atkins and Michael L. Johnson (Lawrence, Kansas: University of Kansas Press, 1985). See also Cynthia Chase, "The Decomposition of the Elephants: Double-Reading *Daniel Deronda*," *PMLA* 93 (1978): 215–27.

18. Kathleen McCormack, *George Eliot's English Travels: Composite characters and coded communication* (New York: Routledge, 2005), p. 2,3.

19. Barbara Hardy, *George Eliot: A Critic's Biography* (London: Continuum, 2006), p. 130.

Further reading

This short selection only begins to reflect the wide range of critical, biographical, and scholarly research on George Eliot. See also chapter 5 "Afterlife" and the footnotes to individual chapters in this volume, as well as the "Further Reading" section of the *Cambridge Companion to George Eliot.*

Biography

Ashton, Rosemary. *G. H. Lewes: A Life.* Oxford: Oxford University Press, 1991.
    George Eliot: A Life. London: Hamish Hamilton, 1996.
Bodenheimer, Rosemarie. *The Real Life of Mary Ann Evans. George Eliot, Her Letters, and Her Fiction.* Ithaca: Cornell University Press, 1994.
Haight, Gordon S. *George Eliot: A Biography.* Oxford: Oxford University Press, 1968.
Hands, Timothy. *A George Eliot Chronology.* Boston: G. K. Hall & Co., 1988.
The George Eliot Letters. 9 vols. Ed. Gordon S. Haight. New Haven: Yale University Press, 1954–5, 1978.
The Journals of George Eliot. Eds. Margaret Harris and Judith Johnstone. Cambridge: Cambridge University Press, 1998.
Lewes, G. H. *The Letters of George Henry Lewes.* 3 Vols. Ed. William Baker. Victoria, BC: University of Victoria Press, 1995/1999.

Collections of reviews and criticism

George Eliot: The Critical Heritage. Ed. David Carroll. London: Routledge and Kegan Paul, 1971.
George Eliot: Critical Assessments. 3 vols. Ed. Stuart Hutchinson. East Sussex: Helm Information Ltd, 1996.
The Cambridge Companion to George Eliot. Ed. George Levine. Cambridge: Cambridge University Press, 2001.
The Oxford Reader's Companion to George Eliot. Ed. John Rignall. Oxford: Oxford University Press, 2000.

General criticism

Baker, William. *George Eliot and Judaism.* Salzburg: Salzburg Studies in English Literature, 1975.

Beer, Gillian. *Darwin's Plots: Evolutionary Narrative in Darwin, George Eliot and Nineteenth-Century Fiction.* London: Ark Paperbacks, 1983.

  George Eliot. Bloomington: Indiana University Press, 1986.

Bonaparte, Felicia. *The Triptych and the Cross: The Central Myths of George Eliot's Poetic Imagination.* New York: New York University Press, 1997.

Carroll, David. *George Eliot and the Conflict of Interpretations.* Cambridge: Cambridge University Press, 1992.

Deirdre David. *Intellectual Women and Victorian Patriarchy: Harriet Martineau, Elizabeth Barrett Browning, George Eliot.* Ithaca: Cornell University Press, 1987.

Dolin, Tim. *George Eliot.* Authors in Context. Oxford: Oxford University Press, 2005.

Gray, Beryl. *George Eliot and Music.* Basingstoke: Macmillan, 1989.

Gilbert, Sandra M. and Susan Gubar. *The Madwoman in the Attic.* New Haven: Yale University Press, 1979.

Graver, Suzanne. *George Eliot and Community: A Study in Social Theory and Fictional Form.* Berkeley: University of California Press, 1984.

Henry, Nancy. *George Eliot and the British Empire.* Cambridge: Cambridge University Press, 2002.

Hertz, Neil. *George Eliot's Pulse.* Stanford: Stanford University Press, 2003.

Knoepflmacher, U. C. *George Eliot's Early Novels: The Limits of Realism.* Berkeley: University of California Press, 1968.

Leavis, F. R. *The Great Tradition: George Eliot, Henry James, Joseph Conrad.* New York: G. W. Stewart, 1949.

Levine, George. *Darwin and the Novelists: Patterns of Science in Victorian Fiction.* Cambridge, MA: Harvard University Press, 1988.

Lewes, G. H. *Versatile Victorian: Selected Writings of George Henry Lewes.* Ed. Rosemary Ashton. Bristol: Bristol Classics Press, 1992.

Newton, K. M. *George Eliot: Romantic Humanist: A Study of the Philosophical Structure of her Novels.* Totowa, New Jersey: Barnes & Noble Books, 1981.

Paris, Bernard J. *Experiments in Life: George Eliot's Quest for Values.* Detroit: Wayne State University Press, 1965.

Paxton, Nancy L. *George Eliot and Herbert Spencer: Feminism, Evolutionism, and the Reconstruction of Gender.* Princeton: Princeton University Press, 1991.

Rignall, John. Ed. *George Eliot and Europe.* Aldershot: Scolar Press, 1997.

Semmel, Bernard. *George Eliot and the Politics of National Inheritance.* Oxford: Oxford University Press, 1994.

Shuttleworth, Sally. *George Eliot and Nineteenth-Century Science.* Cambridge: Cambridge University Press, 1984.

Welsh, Alexander. *George Eliot and Blackmail.* Cambridge, MA: Harvard University Press, 1985.

Whittemeyer, Hugh. *George Eliot and the Visual Arts.* New Haven: Yale University Press, 1979.

Index